NOT FOR CIRCULATION

THE WORLD'S BEST THIN BOOKS

What to Read When Your Book Report Is Due Tomorrow

New ^ Edition
Thinner

Joni Richards Bodart

The Scarecrow Press, Inc.
Lanham, Maryland, and London
2000

SCARECROW PRESS, INC.

Published in the United States of America
by Scarecrow Press, Inc.
4720 Boston Way, Lanham, Maryland 20706
http://www.scarecrowpress.com

4 Pleydell Gardens, Folkestone
Kent CT20 2DN, England

British Library Cataloguing in Publication Information Available

Library of Congress Cataloging-in-Publication Data
Bodart, Joni Richards.
    The world's best thin books : what to read when your book
report is due tomorrow / Joni Richards Bodart. — Rev. abridged ed.
        p.   cm.
    Rev. abridged ed. of : 100 world-class thin books. 1993.
    Includes bibliographical references and index.
    ISBN 1-57886-007-5 (pbk. : alk. paper)
    I. Bodart, Joni Richards. 100 world-class thin books. II. Title.
    Z1037 .B66 2000 PN1009.A1
    028.1'62—dc21   99-38615
                                                        CIP

☉™ The paper used in this publication meets the minimum requirements of
American National Standard for Information Sciences—Permanence of
Paper for Printed Library Materials, ANSI/NISO Z39.48–1992.
Manufactured in the United States of America.

To Patty, Cathi, and Martha—

For all you've done, for all you are,
And for all we are together.
Thanks for making the "hardly possible"
A wonderful reality!

"One friend in a lifetime is much; two are many; three are hardly possible."
—Henry Brooks Adams (1838–1918)
The Education of Henry Adams, 1907

📖 CONTENTS 📖

THINNEST

THINNER

THIN

📖 Acknowledgments for the Revised Edition 📖

This is the book I was sure would never happen, and I want to acknowledge the people who helped make it a reality. First, Shirley Lambert, who saw its potential and encouraged me to make the necessary changes to update the original material. I look forward to working with her on numerous books in the future.

My circle of family and friends have, as always, been patient and supportive during the creative process. I am particularly grateful to my computer guru, my cousin Patty Comer, whose calm responses to my frantic phone calls helped me through more than one crisis, whether they involved computers or not, and who took me away from the computer ("Hi! Let's do lunch—I just discovered a new restaurant!") when my stress level went over the top. Teresa Burkert and Mildred Hall, Branch Manager and Senior Librarian, respectively, at the Woodbury Branch of the Denver Public Library, let me take two weeks off on very short notice so I could finish typesetting the manuscript *almost* on time. Teresa's weekly question, "How's the book doing, Joni?" has become a familiar refrain during the last few months. I appreciate their friendship and support very much, just as I do the interest and support I have received from the rest of the Woodbury-Smiley family. Thanks, gang—*you're all great!*

Then there are the friends, old and new, who help keep me sane and centered, even when my life is at its most chaotic—Patty Campbell, the best bestgirlfriend anyone could ever have, Jim Heiser, still a good friend, shared his paper and printer with me (the final camera-ready copy was made on his printer), Cathi MacRae and Martha Franklin, long-distance friends who make me grateful for E-mail, and Floyd (Laff) Lafferty, new friend, generous dispenser of encouragement, laughter, and hugs, who spent long, boring weekends proofing the final manuscript and helping me put together the table of contents and the indexes, a job that was far more massive than those few words can convey!

Thank you, thank you, one and all. There's no doubt in my mind that I couldn't make it without you!

—Joni Richards Bodart

📖 Acknowledgments 📖

Many people contributed to this book in a variety of ways. Patty Campbell suggested that Libraries Unlimited contact me when they asked her who she thought would like to write it. David Loertscher and Martha Franklin caught me up in their enthusiasm about it and helped me see it as a book that I wanted to write.

A group of dedicated school and public librarians took time from their busy schedules to first talk to me and then to send in their ideas about which titles should be included and which omitted. Thanks to all of them: Joan Atkinson, Stella Baker, Jane Chandra, Beryl Eber, Marion Hargrove, Patrick Jones, Lyn Knapp, Cathi Mac-Rae, Susan Madden, Hazel Rochman, Helen Tallman, Debbie Taylor, Barbara Thorngren, Diane Tuccillo, Laura Weber, and Lynda Welborn. People also sent in lists of thin books from the following library systems: Alameda County Library (California), New York Public Library, Los Angeles Public Library, Prince George's County Memorial Library (Maryland), Cuyahoga County Public Library (Ohio), Contra Costa County Library (California), Springfield City Library (Illinois), Mesa Public Library (Arizona), King County Public Library (Washington), Cherry Creek Schools (Englewood, Colorado), and Irving Intermediate School (Texas).

I also appreciate the assistance of the reference staff at the Columbine Branch of the Jefferson County Public Library (Colorado) for helping me verify bibliographic data and also filling what seemed to me to be hundreds of requests for books I needed to read, frequently on short notice, before deciding whether to include them or not.

I would also be remiss to omit the friends and family that encouraged me and helped me keep going when the going was somewhat less than easy. First and foremost, my closest circle of friends who both prodded and encouraged me, and some of whom set examples for me by sticking to their own deadlines: Patty Campbell, Cathi MacRae, Martha Franklin, and Harry Madden. When I stayed with my mother, Frances Noble, for several weeks after surgery, she put up with a computer always set up on her dining table, stacks of books everywhere, and a daughter who preferred quiet to company while she worked.

And, finally, I want to say thanks to the students in the classes I visited in Florida and Colorado who, when I told them what book I was working on, immediately picked up their pencils to jot down the name and inquired anxiously about when it would be available.

Thanks to all of you for the encouragement, the reminders, the feedback, the work, and the support each of you contributed. As always, I could not have done it without you.

—Joni Richards Bodart

📖 Introduction for Students 📖

I wonder just exactly why you picked up this book: You don't like to read? You don't have time to read a long book for class with all the other things you're interested in? You forgot that you had a book report due until just a few minutes ago? It's getting to the end of the semester, and you need some extra credit to make up for that home-work you blew off or the test you didn't study for?

Well, whatever the reason is, I hope you'll find some help for your problem in this book. But that doesn't mean that I'm going to tell you enough about a book to let you get by without reading it! I want to make these books sound so exciting and interesting that you won't mind spending a couple of hours or an evening meeting the people I want to introduce you to in these books.

What you'll find in this book are lists of characters in books, booktalks that give you a "commercial" for each of the books, and ideas on how you might start writing a book report or a booktalk on each of the titles. I've also included indexes, so you can find out which books would be best to use in certain classes or what books are about your favorite subjects. My hope is that *The World's Best Thin Books* has enough information to get you started but does not do all the work for you.

All the books I'm going to be talking about have three things in common: They are all 200 pages or less in length; they are all suit-able for middle- and high-school students; and they are all good books. How do I know? I had to read each of them, usually more than once, and then spend time writing about each of them. If I thought a book wasn't interesting, I left it out. Not that you'll necessarily like every book you find here. But there should be at least a few that will catch your attention. And if you think I've left out some really good thin books or included some real dogs, please let me know. I'd love to hear from you—who knows, there may be another edition of this book some day, with another hundred titles that are good, fast reading! You can E-mail me at jonibr@yahoo.com.

I've included all the information I hope you'll need to get started in the right direction. But the rest is up to you.

Have fun, and happy reading!

📖 Introduction for Librarians and Teachers 📖

Does the thought of dealing with just one more teenager wanting the thinnest possible book for that dreaded, long-put-off and now-imminent book report make you want to scream with frustration? If so, perhaps this book can relieve your frustration and help you cope with students' requests for thin books.

Here you'll find information on 94 titles selected by a group of school and public librarians. These titles are less than 200 pages in length, of interest to middle- and high-school students, and include some of the best examples of short novels for adolescents and young adults.

Each entry includes information on subject areas, characters, major themes, and ideas for writing a book report or booktalk. The ideas on how to write a book report or booktalk may refer to themes or characters not mentioned elsewhere. Therefore, by comparing entries on titles and students' work, it should be easy to determine if they have actually read the book or not.

Indexes cover subject and curriculum areas and genres, as well as authors and titles. The books are arranged alphabetically in three sections—thinnest, thinner, and thin.

My goal is to make this book a useful resource to you and the students you serve. If you know of titles that should have been included (currently in print and 200 pages or less in length in paperback, if paperback is available), I hope you will let me know what they are. My E-mail address is jonirb@yahoo.com. There's always the possibility that another edition will be forthcoming and that I'll do it all again!

📖 How to Use This Book 📖

This book is a quick reference guide to 94 short novels (all under 200 pages in length). You'll find a lot of information about these books before you even pick one up. This guide will help you determine what novels you may want to read, either for fun or for a school assignment.

Ninety-four novels may seem like a lot to choose from, but you can easily narrow down the choices. First, consider what *type* of novels you like—historical fiction or romances, humor or suspense. Use the genre index to guide you to the kind of book you want to read. Next, think of what topics interest you. The subject index lists dozens of subjects, from adoption to writing, divorce to time travel. Perhaps you don't have time to read a complicated novel, or maybe you want a book you can really sink your teeth into. The readability index will guide you to the "quick reads" or "thoughtful" novels. If you have a favorite author or already know of a novel you want to read, check the author or title index. If you are looking for a book for a particular class, check the curriculum index.

Once you find some titles that interest you, look at each entry. The top of each listing has the title, author, and publishing information, as well as the book's grade level, suitable curriculum areas, the readability of the book, and the genre. Read the booktalk next to find out whether the book is really one you want to read.

After you've read the book, look at the ideas and themes section. It will provide a good starting point for writing your book report or booktalk. Don't forget to read the tips in the appendixes for more help in writing your report or talk. If you use these ideas to guide you, you'll find that writing that book report or booktalk is a lot easier than you thought it would be!

📖 Key Terms & Abbreviations 📖

CURRICULUM AREA
Am Hist = American History
Archaeology
Art = The Arts: Dancing,
    Sculpture, Painting, etc.
Astron = Astronomy
Creat Writing = Creative Writing
Drama
Eng = English
Ethics
For Lang = Foreign Language
Geog = Geography
Govt = Government
Home Ec = Home Economics
Jour = Journalism
Music
PE = Physical Education
Psych = Psychology
Sci = Science
Sex Ed = Sex Education
Soc Studies = Social Studies
Sociology
Voc Ed = Vocational Education
W Hist = World History
Writing

GRADE LEVEL
HS = high school
JH = middle school/junior
    high school

GENRE
Adventure
Classic fiction
Fantasy
Historical fiction
Humor
Horror
Mystery
Realistic fiction
Romance
Science fiction
Supernatural
Suspense
Western

READABILITY
Quick read
Average
Thoughtful

PUBLISHING INFORMATION
pb = paperback

THINNEST

📖 THINNEST 📖

THE GHOSTS OF DEPARTURE POINT. Eve Bunting. Scholastic, 1982, 114p., $2.25(pb); Harper & Row, 1982, 113p., $12.70. JH, HS. Eng, PE. Quick read; supernatural, romance.

SUBJECT AREAS
Death and dying; Friendship; Family relationships.

CHARACTERS
Vicki West: a cheerleader who dies in a car crash at Departure Point and returns to the scene of her death as a ghost.

Ted Clark: a teenager who is killed at Departure Point about a year after Vicki's death and also returns as a ghost.

Rebecca: a young woman who, along with her son, is killed when a defective tire on their car blows out. As a ghost, she is determined to save others from her fate.

Mary Draper, Susan Wu, Carla Sanchez: Vicki's best friends and fellow cheerleaders, who are killed with her in the crash at Departure Point.

BOOKTALK
Vicki knew from the beginning that the wreck had been her fault. She and three other cheerleaders, her best friends, were on the way home after a game to change for the big dance. Everyone was excited, and Vicki was clowning around in the back seat, shaking her pompoms in the driver's face. The car went out of control, and all four of them died.

When Vicki woke up, she was a ghost, alone, condemned to haunt the place where she and her friends died. Departure Point was the deadliest stretch of road in the area, a sharp curve where more than one car had crashed to the rocks below. Vicki could see and hear the living, but they could neither see nor hear her. Sometimes she was so lonely she went back to her home at night to sleep in her own bed and hear her parents talking about her. She wished with all her heart that she could go back and change the past and live, or find a way to die and be at peace, but she couldn't.

Vicki was neither the first nor the last person to die at Departure Point. A year after her death, it claimed its thirteenth victim, Ted Clark. Like Vicki, Ted caused the accident that killed him. Also like Vicki, he wasn't the only one to die in that wreck. He'd been at a wedding and offered the maid of honor a ride home, even though he knew he'd had too much to drink. Now Ted is also a ghost, condemned to haunt the place where he died.

They became friends, and spent all their time together. For the first time since she died, Vicki was happy. But after meeting another ghost haunting the Point, they realized that the only way they could go on and be at peace was to atone for what they had done. Somehow they had to convince the town council to build a new and safer highway, so that Departure Point would not claim any more innocent lives. But how could two ghosts, invisible to everyone but each other, convince the living to do anything? And Vicki wasn't even sure she wanted to leave Departure Point.

Yes, she and Ted would be at peace, but would that be worth the price—never seeing him again?

MAJOR IDEAS OR THEMES
Sometimes it may be necessary to do good in order to atone for the bad things one has done.

If you get a second chance to make something right, it is important not to repeat the same mistake.

BOOK REPORT IDEAS
1. Describe what all the ghosts in this book have in common and why they have become ghosts instead of just vanishing.
2. Discuss the idea of atonement as it is described in this book, showing how "balancing the scales" allows the ghosts to go free.
3. At the end of the book, when Vicki finds herself in the car with her friends, she feels that she has been through the experience once before. This is commonly called "déjà vu." Discuss other situations that might produce this feeling and why.

BOOKTALK IDEAS
1. Write your talk as if you were Vicki, revealing only in the last sentence that she is a ghost.
2. Have each of the main characters tell his or her story of how they happened to be at Departure Point.

📖 📖 📖

GRUEL AND UNUSUAL PUNISHMENT. Jim Arter. Delacorte, 1991, 103p., $13.95. JH, HS. Eng, Soc Studies. Quick read; realistic fiction, humor.

SUBJECT AREAS
School; Friendship; Mental illness.

CHARACTERS
Arnold Dinklighter (Dink): a seventh-grade prankster who spends much of his time in detention.

Edward Straight: Arnold's friend and fellow prankster. He may be starting to take their pranks too seriously.

Mr. Applin: the detention teacher, who calls his room "the Gulag" and stresses the importance of homework. Arnold and Edward call him "Apeface."

Mrs. Dinklighter: Arnold's mother. She is more than a little crazy, a fact that Arnold works hard at keeping secret.

Miss Carmichael: the English teacher, who is the butt of many of Arnold's jokes.

Mr. Workman: the school principal.

Susan Winkerman: a pretty but not overly intelligent student whose locker is next to Arnold's. He teases her a lot.

BOOKTALK
Have you ever had a teacher you really hated? Someone you wished would just disappear into thin air? That's how Arnold felt about Mr. Applin— also known as "Apeface"—especially after Apeface flunked him in history, forcing him to repeat the seventh grade. There wasn't anything Arnold could do about it, either, except to make everyone at school as sorry to be around him as he was to be there. And that's exactly what he did. As a result, no one liked him—not the other kids, not the teachers, and not the principal, who was getting tired of finding Arnold in his office every time he turned around.

But all anyone knew about Arnold was the way he acted at school. No one knew what it was like for him at home, where his crazy mother left him to take care of himself because she was pretty much out of it all the time. Arnold had gotten used to things being that way. He liked it, even if he did get lonely some-times. But even if he'd wanted the other kids to be more friendly, he couldn't take the chance of letting anyone find out about his mother. If they did, they'd take him away from her, and since his dad had left, she was all he had.

Then Edward moved to town. Edward talked to Arnold. He even wanted to be his friend. Now Arnold had a partner to play jokes with and to help him while away the time in "the Gulag." Slowly, though, Arnold was beginning to realize that Edward was even crazier than Arnold's mother, and that when Edward said, "Let's get Apeface," he meant it. So far Arnold had just been kidding. Did he really want to get serious now?

MAJOR IDEAS OR THEMES

Teachers are human beings, too.

No one likes a practical joker who can't be serious once in a while.

Appearances and actions can be deceiving.

Each person must take responsibility for him or herself.

No one can help people who aren't willing to help themselves.

When a joke goes too far, it becomes serious.

BOOK REPORT IDEAS

1. Discuss the meaning of "the Gulag" and how Mr. Applin was acting as one of the guards. Include both Arnold's and Mr. Applin's points of view about detention hall, its purpose, and how it was carried out. Compare it to a real gulag.
2. Describe Mr. Applin from Arnold's point of view and from the point of view of one of his other students, perhaps Susan Winkerman. Show what kind of a teacher he was and why. Include your own opinion of him and whether you would like to have him as a teacher.
3. Arnold was a hard person to get to know. Explain why and discuss what you might have done to make friends with him. How could you have gotten past the facade he showed to the real person inside? Which character or characters in the book knew the most about who Arnold really was?
4. Discuss the purpose of Arnold's practical jokes. Which characters saw through him?

BOOKTALK IDEAS

1. Become Arnold and tell the story in the first person.
2. Using the first person, tell the story from Susan's point of view. Make sure you include only information about Arnold that she knows.
3. Make Arnold's practical jokes the focus of your talk, mentioning several briefly and telling about your favorite in detail.
4. Write a short talk, mentioning only the Gulag, Apeface, and Arnold's pranks.

THE LITTLE PRINCE. Antoine de Saint-Exupery. Harcourt, Brace, Jovanovich, 1968, 112p., $3.95(pb); Harcourt, Brace, Jovanovich, 1943, 91p., $12.95. JH, HS. Eng, Psych, Sociology. Quick read; fantasy, classic fiction.

SUBJECT AREAS
Philosophy; Art; Friendship; Love.

CHARACTERS
The Little Prince: a boy who lives on an asteroid and tends a beautiful flower. Hurt by the flower's selfishness, he leaves the asteroid and goes on a journey among the planets.

The Pilot: an airplane pilot who meets the Little Prince in the desert and tries to help him by drawing pictures. He and the Little Prince become good friends.

The King, the Conceited Man, the Tippler, the Businessman, the Lamplighter, and the Geographer: people whom the Little Prince meets along the way.

The Fox: a teacher who shows the Little Prince the secret of what is truly important in life.

BOOKTALK
Once upon a time there was a Little Prince who lived on an asteroid. The asteroid was also home to a beautiful flower, which the Little Prince tended faithfully for a long time. The flower was very selfish, however, and eventually she made the Little Prince so unhappy that he decided to leave the asteroid and go traveling. After many adventures, he met a fox who showed him what it meant to truly love his flower, a pilot who wrote down his story, and a snake who showed him how to get home.

Perhaps that is all you will find in this story. That is all that grown-ups, or at least most grown-ups, find. But perhaps you are not yet completely grown up. Perhaps you will find much, much more. If you do, then you are one of the lucky ones.

MAJOR IDEAS OR THEMES
You must first understand something before you can truly love it.

Loving something makes you responsible for it.

The most precious gifts are the ones you have taken the time and trouble to create.

A person has the right to disobey an unreasonable order.

Judging oneself requires true wisdom.
If you are lucky enough to have a friend, you should value and remember that friend as long as you can.

BOOK REPORT IDEAS
1. Explain the basic allegorical lesson taught in this book and why you think the author wrote it.
2. The various characters the Little Prince meets on his travels give him bits of their thinking or philosophy. Discuss these ideas and organize them into a cohesive structure.
3. Discuss what this story means to you and which of the bits of philosophy mean the most to you and why.
4. Examine the view of grown-ups in the book, starting with the dedication page, and show whether you agree with it.

BOOKTALK IDEAS
1. Write a talk from the point of view of the Little Prince. Explain why he left his home and what he saw and learned.
2. Write your talk from the point of view of the pilot, showing how he met the Little Prince and became his friend.

THE NIGHT THE WHITE DEER DIED. Gary Paulsen. Dell, 1991, 105p., $3.50(pb). JH, HS. Eng, Soc Studies, Art. Quick read; realistic fiction, adventure.

SUBJECT AREAS
Native Americans; Rites of passage; Family relationships.

CHARACTERS
Janet Carson: a tall, graceful 15-year-old with long brown hair. She keeps having the same dream, one that causes her to wake up terrified, in a cold sweat.

Billy Honcho: an old Native American who spends his time drinking and sleeping it off in the Plaza.

Janet's mother: a sculptor who loves her daughter and struggles to understand her.

BOOKTALK
For reasons she doesn't understand, 15-year-old Janet feels drawn to Billy Honcho, an old Native American who sleeps off his drunken binges in the Plaza. Maybe it has something to do with the dream she has over and over—a dream of a white doe and a warrior dressed all in white, who is drawing his bow to shoot the deer. Janet always wakes up before the deer is hit, until the night Billy comes to her house on a horse, dressed all in white and leading a pony, and asks her to ride away with him. That night, she hears the stories of his people. That night, she learns who he might have been. That night, the white deer dies.

MAJOR IDEAS OR THEMES
Sometimes beautiful things appear ugly, and sometimes ugly things are only waiting for beauty to happen to them.

People sometimes connect with each other in ways that others cannot understand or accept.

Sometimes we must simply accept what happens to us without trying to understand or analyze it.

BOOK REPORT IDEAS
1. Describe in your own words what this story is saying and what it means to you.
2. What was Billy's message to Janet—why did he ride with her and tell her his stories? What did he want from her? What did she get from him?
3. Describe the role Janet's mother played in Janet's relationship with Billy and why you think her mother acted the way she did.

BOOKTALK IDEAS
1. Focus on Janet's dream and how it led her to make friends with Billy.
2. Write a character description talk describing Janet and the Indian man she sees first in her dreams and then in reality—but don't give away who the man really is or what he means to her.

📖 📖 📖

SAVE QUEEN OF SHEBA. Louise Moeri. Avon, 1990, 112p., $2.95(pb); Dutton, 1981, 116p., $14.95. JH, HS. Soc Studies, Am Hist, Eng, Psych. Quick read; historical fiction, adventure.

SUBJECT AREAS
Survival; Family relationships; Self-knowledge.

CHARACTERS
King David: a 12-year-old boy who has been traveling with a wagon train. Half-scalped and left for dead by Sioux warriors, he must figure out how to save himself and his little sister.

Queen of Sheba: David's 6-year-old sister. Frail, spoiled, and uncooperative, she is more of a hindrance than a help to her brother.

BOOKTALK
When King David woke up, the first thing he saw was a huge greenish black fly crawling along his hand, just in front of his face. He took a breath and felt searing pain in his head. He sat up carefully and looked around. He saw an overturned wagon with a dead man beneath it, smashed water kegs, and lots of bodies—horses, women, children, all with arrows sticking out of them.

Slowly he got to his feet and felt his head, which throbbed with pain. He seemed to be half-scalped, but he was alive. King David thought he was the only person left alive by the Sioux raiding party, until he found his little sister, Queen of Sheba. Now it was up to him to see that they caught up with the rest of the wagon train and their parents. He took stock of their resources—a little water, some raw cornmeal, a tiny piece of bacon, some apples, a gun, and a few shells. They were alone on the prairie with only each other to depend on—a 12-year-old boy who was almost delirious from loss of blood and the infection in his wound, and a stubborn, spoiled 6-year-old brat who refused to do anything he asked.

Before they'd gone very far, they found one of the wagon train's horses caught in some bushes, and a clear-flowing stream where they could get water and David could wash his head. Now at least they had a chance, he thought—if only he could keep his patience and his wits about him and figure out a way to put up with Queen of Sheba and her demands until they could catch up with the wagon train.

MAJOR IDEAS OR THEMES
How you win is as important as winning itself.

You can survive against great odds if you think before you act.

When you're struggling to survive, you may need to use everything you ever learned to stay alive.

In a confrontation, it is possible for both parties to win.

Keeping your goal in your mind will help you reach it.

BOOK REPORT IDEAS
1. Use the descriptions in the book to draw a map showing the most likely route for King David and Queen of Sheba.
2. Compare what King David and Queen of Sheba had to do to survive to a similar situation in today's world. What might two children on their own—without anyone to help them and only minimal food and water— have to do to survive in today's world? What survival skills would they need?
3. Discuss the concept of winning as it is explained in the book, and describe the ways in which King David both won and lost as he struggled to keep himself and his little sister alive.
4. Discuss the meaning of the final sentence in the book, citing quotes to support your view.
5. How do you think this experience affected the way King David and Queen of Sheba lived the rest of their lives? Remember they would have both positive and negative memories and mental as well as physical scars.
6. Discuss the significance of the children's names.

BOOKTALK IDEAS
1. Write your talk in the first person, speaking as King David. Describe how you feel when you wake up and realize you and your sister are on your own in the wilderness.
2. Write your talk in the first person, speaking as Queen of Sheba. Describe how you feel about being abandoned and having to depend on your older brother. You can be as bratty as the character in the book.
3. Write a character description booktalk, focusing on who King David is and then who Queen of Sheba is. Draw your information from the whole book, but be careful not to give away anything. Describe, compare, and contrast the two children, ending with a question or two about whether they have a chance of survival.

📖 📖 📖

SING DOWN THE MOON. Scott O'Dell. Dell, 1976, 138p., $2.95(pb). JH. Soc Studies, Sociology. Quick read; historical fiction, adventure, romance.

SUBJECT AREAS
Crime and delinquency; Native Americans; Racism; Friendship; Death and dying; Kidnapping; Survival; Family relationships; Self-knowledge.

CHARACTERS
Bright Morning: a 15-year-old Navajo sheepherder who is captured by Spanish slavers and taken away from her family and friends.

Running Bird: Bright Morning's friend who is also captured by the Spaniards.

White Deer: another friend of Bright Morning. She also herds sheep.

Tall Boy: the young man whom Bright Morning wants to marry. He is wounded trying to rescue her.

Rosita: a slave who urges Bright Morning to forget her family and her home.

Nehana: another slave who helps Bright Morning and Running Bird escape.

Bitter Water: a medicine man and healer who is unable to heal Tall Boy's wounded shoulder.

BOOKTALK
Bright Morning had everything a young Navajo woman could ever ask for—a beautiful home, a loving family, good friends, her own herd of sheep, and soon, if she was lucky, a wonderful husband. All of this changed the morning she and Running Bird were captured by Spanish slavers and taken far from their home. It would be many weeks before they would see their friends and families again. When Tall Boy, Bright Morning's intended husband, tried to rescue them, he was shot in the shoulder. Even Bitter Water, the tribe's medicine man, could not heal him, and without the use of his right arm, Tall Boy could no longer be a warrior and protect his people from danger.

And danger was coming. One day United States soldiers arrived and told Bright Morning's people that they had to leave their canyon home and go with them. When the tribe refused, the soldiers destroyed their homes, their crops, and their orchard. After that, they had no choice but to leave; they followed the soldiers, not knowing what lay ahead.

What will happen to Bright Morning's dreams? Will any of them ever come true? Will she ever see her canyon and her sheep again, or hear her children's laughter echo off the tall canyon walls?

Find out as you follow her and her fellow Navajos on the Long Walk.

MAJOR IDEAS OR THEMES
It is sometimes necessary to fight in order to survive.

Food and a warm bed are not sufficient reason to sacrifice your heritage and your freedom.

When you love someone enough, it doesn't matter whether or not that person is whole in body or spirit.

Hold fast to your dreams and you may achieve them.

BOOK REPORT IDEAS
1.   Describe the way Bright Morning changed during the course of the book and the things she learned that helped her to survive.
2.   Discuss the Indians' view of the white soldiers and settlers, their customs, their justice, and the way they took over the Indians' lands.
3.   Discuss the relationship between Bright Morning and Tall Boy and how it changed over time, especially after he was wounded. How do you think their life together would have differed, or not differed, if they had been a white rather than a Navajo couple?

BOOKTALK IDEAS
1.   Focus your talk on the Long Walk and on how the white people treated the Indians.
2.   Write a character description talk that focuses on Bright Morning.
3.   Using the scene or anecdote technique, center your talk on one of the major scenes in the book, for instance, when Bright Morning and Running Bird are captured by Spanish slavers or when Tall Boy is injured rescuing them.

📖 📖 📖

VISION QUEST. Pamela Service. Fawcett, 1990, 120p., $2.95(pb); Macmillan, 1989, 160p.$12.95. JH, HS. Archaeology, Am Hist. Thoughtful; supernatural, adventure.

SUBJECT AREAS
American history; Time travel; Family relationships; Friendship; Native Americans; Death and dying.

CHARACTERS

Kate Elliot: a teenager who has spent her life moving from one army base to another. When her father dies, she and her mother move to a small town on the edge of the desert.

Mrs. Elliot: Kate's mother, the curator for the local museum.

Uncle Bernie: Mrs. Elliot's uncle.

Pete: a pothunter who steals the shaman's stone from the archaeological site where it belonged.

Jimmy Fong: a friend of Kate's who plans to be an archaeologist.

Hizu: a shaman who lived in the pueblo in ancient times.

Wadat: Hizu's apprentice.

BOOKTALK

It was just a stone—smooth, black, and tapered at both ends, with a single carved line spiraling down its length. Kate ran her fingers along the groove, thinking of the person who had carved it so long ago. Suddenly she seemed to see him before her, holding the stone in his hand, gazing at her across the centuries that divided them. Then he was gone, and instead she saw Pete, the pothunter who had looted the site of the ancient pueblo and who was demanding that she return the stone he considered his property. But she couldn't bring herself to let go of it. Abruptly he snatched it out of her hand. A sudden swirling light blinded her, and she felt a wrenching sense of loss, a loss so great she almost cried with the pain of it.

Kate didn't realize it at first, but the stone was a charm stone, one that belonged to a wise and powerful shaman who had lived centuries ago. But it wasn't until she found a second charm stone, a red one with three carved lines, that she began to realize the power of the stones. With them, she traveled back in time to the days when the pueblo was a thriving village and met the two men who had carved them. Now the shaman and his apprentice had a task for her to accomplish. It was up to her to discover what it was and how to do it. If she failed, their lives—and hers—would never be the same again.

Long ago, the shaman and his apprentice had gone on their vision quest. Now, Kate must go on hers.

MAJOR IDEAS OR THEMES

Magic endures through time.

In helping others, we help ourselves.

Evil deeds will eventually be punished.

Loved ones who have gone live on in our memories of them.

Magic is hidden from those who can't respond to it.

If you find your true path in life, pursue it with zeal and determination.

BOOK REPORT IDEAS
1.   Discuss the idea that time is a river and that entering it at different points can take us to other times and places.
2.   Compare Wadat and Kate; how they are alike and how they are different.
3.   At the end of the book, Kate says she feels at peace, just as Wadat and Hizu do. Show how she changed during the course of the novel and what factors contributed to that feeling of peace.
4.   Compare the concept of the shaman's charm stone to good-luck charms a modern person might own, and show what functions these modern-day "charm stones" might have.
5.   The mood, or the gestalt, of the book is based upon Native American philosophies about life and death. Discuss those ideas and how they affected you as the reader.
6.   Discuss what you believe to be the most powerful idea in the book, the one that affected you the most.

BOOKTALK IDEAS
1.   Write your talk as if you were Wadat seeing his spirit person for the first time.
2.   Use both Kate and Wadat's words to bring both of their worlds to life.
3.   Use a picture of a charm stone similar to one of those in the book to illustrate your talk.
4.   Focus your talk on the idea of charm stones and how Kate and Jimmy responded to them.

📖 📖 📖

WEETZIE BAT. Francesca Lia Block. HarperCollins, 1990, 88p., $3.50(pb); HarperCollins, 1989, 96p., $12.95. HS. Eng, Psych. Quick read; fantasy, romance, supernatural, humor.

SUBJECT AREAS
Family relationships; Unwed mothers; Friendship; Homosexuality; Death and dying.

CHARACTERS
Weetzie Bat: a teenage girl who wears her bleached-blond hair in a flattop and loves to dress in wild, cool clothes.

Dirk: Weetzie's best friend.

Duck: Dirk's lover who appears as a result of Weetzie's wish.

My Secret Agent Lover Man: Weetzie's lover who also appears as a result of her wish.

Grandma Fifi: Dirk's grandmother who wills her cottage to Weetzie and Dirk when she dies.

Slinkster Dog: Weetzie's dog.

Go-go Girl: a girlfriend for Slinkster.

Charlie Bat: Weetzie's father.

Brandy-Lynn Bat: Weetzie's mother.

BOOKTALK
Weetzie Bat had bleached-blond hair cut in a flattop, and she wore pink Harlequin glasses and strawberry lipstick. She lived in the city that was hot and cool, glum and slam, glitter and glitz, where all your dreams could come true if you believed in them enough—L.A. Weetzie's best friend, Dirk, had a black shoe-polish Mohawk and drove a cool red '55 Pontiac. Dirk and Weetzie went everywhere together, and every night they came back to the cottage where Dirk lived with his grandmother and told her all about their adventures and everything they had seen.

But one day, they told Grandma Fifi that they were sad. "We want Ducks," Dirk said. "Two someones to care about us and love us, so we can live happily ever after." You see, Dirk was gay, and even though he and Weetzie were best friends, they both wanted something more, something they couldn't give each other. So Grandma Fifi thought about it, and when Weetzie left to go home, she gave her a beautiful golden object covered with dust. At home, when Weetzie started to rub the dust off, out came a genie who offered her three wishes. Sure enough, all Weetzie's wishes came true—mostly—which is how she and Dirk discovered that getting your wishes granted doesn't necessarily mean living happily ever after, and that real life is a lot different than life in the movies—and that's okay.

MAJOR IDEAS OR THEMES
When you find someone you really love, it's worth the time and energy it takes to make the relationship work.

You don't have to be like everyone else to be happy—enjoy being different if that's who you are.

Loving someone includes forgiving them when they hurt you or make you angry.

Friendship is just as important as romantic love.

Just because two people are different doesn't mean they can't be friends.

BOOK REPORT IDEAS
1.   Tell a fairy tale based on this book, written in the style of traditional fairy tales.
2.   Describe how this book is like real life and how it is different.
3.   Tell what you think happened after this book was over.
4.   Explain what you think "happily ever after" means in real life.
5.   Write a different ending for this book and explain why you think it is as good as the ending in the book.
6.   This story is set in Los Angeles. If you think it could be set anywhere else, describe where it would be and how that location would change or not change the characters. If you think it could only happen in L.A., explain why.

BOOKTALK IDEAS
1.   Let Weetzie tell her own story in her own words, leading up to a climax. You decide how much or how little to tell.
2.   Tell the story as if it were a fairy tale.
3.   This book has an unusual writing style. Use this style in your talk to make the story come alive, and let your audience know what to expect from the book.

📖 📖 📖

WHICHAWAY. Glendon Swarthout and Kathryn Swarthout. Knopf, 1966, 101p., $3.50(pb). JH. Eng, Am Hist. Quick read; realistic fiction, western.

SUBJECT AREAS
Survival; Working; Family relationships; Self-knowledge; Crime and delinquency.

CHARACTERS
Whichaway: a teenager who spends his summers on his father's ranch with the hired hands and his winters with a family in town. He knows that his father doesn't approve of him.

Beans: the ranch cook who keeps an eye on Whichaway.

Dub: Whichaway's horse.

Whichaway's father: owner of the Box O Ranch. He makes his son live in the bunkhouse in an attempt to toughen him up.

BOOKTALK
When there is no one to depend on for survival except yourself, it's your own fault if you die. But Whichaway is determined to survive. He got himself into this situation, and he will get himself out. Maybe if he does, his father will finally be proud of him.

But how is he going to do it? He's 30 feet above the ground, on a small platform on the top of a windmill, with two broken legs—and no one has any idea where he is. No one will come looking for him before tomorrow morning at the earliest. Beans, the ranch cook, expects him to be at the windmill near Crittendon's because that's where Whichaway said he was going. Instead, he's at Crazy Man Mesa, a long ride from the ranch house. He has no food, no water, and no way to get down. The only people who have come by are two rustlers who left him to die, and a crazy old prospector who tried to kill him to keep him from revealing the location of a big gold strike.

Can a skinny 15-year-old boy with no resources but his wits and his determination survive for days in the hot Arizona sun? Will he make it back to the ranch house, or will he die all alone on top of the windmill?

MAJOR IDEAS OR THEMES
When you have only yourself to depend on for survival, you had better keep your wits about you.

A single impulsive act can change your life—or end it.

With determination and a willingness to think things through, you can accomplish almost anything.

When no one cares for you, you learn to care for yourself.

BOOK REPORT IDEAS

1.   Discuss how Whichaway's life has prepared him for the challenge he faces on Crazy Man Mesa.

2.   The relationship between Whichaway and his father is one of the central themes of the book. Describe that relationship and show how you think it will or will not change as a result of Whichaway's ordeal. If you think it is possible for Whichaway to change his father's mind about him, show what you think he would have to do to bring this about.

3.   Speculate on what kind of man you think Whichaway will become and how his ordeal on the windmill will affect his adult life. How do you think he will relate to his father as an adult? Will it differ from the way he relates to him as a child?

4.   Discuss the last comments Whichaway makes to himself on the way back to the ranch house (the next to the last paragraph in the book.) How will they change his life that summer and in the future?

BOOKTALK IDEAS

1.   Focus your talk on one of the scenes you found most exciting, for example, when Whichaway broke his legs, his experience with the rustlers or with the prospector, or how he made a "rope" to help him get down.

2.   Describe Whichaway's life, leading up to his decision to go to the mesa and the accident that broke his legs.

3.   Focus your talk on the idea of survival and how Whichaway manages to save his own life.

THE WINTER ROOM. Gary Paulsen. Orchard, 1989, 103p., $11.95. JH, HS. Eng, Am Hist, Psych. Quick read; realistic fiction.

SUBJECT AREAS

Family relationships; Self-knowledge; Working.

CHARACTERS

Eldon: the 11-year-old narrator of the story and a keen observer of all that goes on at his family's farm.

Wayne: Eldon's know-it-all 13-year-old brother.

Mother: a farmer's wife whose life consists of keeping house, helping to run the farm, and tending anyone who is sick.

Father: a big, quiet man who cares about his farm almost as much as he cares about his wife and sons.

Uncle David: Eldon's great-uncle who tells stories in the winter as the family sits by the fire.

Nels: an old farm hand who works hard and says little.

BOOKTALK

Life on the farm is much the same from year to year. In spring, the snow melts and the manure pile gives off a choking smell. Summer is a time for plowing, haying, threshing—and picnics. Fall is the killing time, when pigs scream and red blood flows until it seems as though the farm is covered with it.

And in winter, when no work can be done outdoors, our family spends the evenings sitting around the stove in what I call the winter room—Mother, Father, Uncle David, Nels, Wayne and I. Sometimes Uncle David tells stories—stories from his past or of Viking adventures. The stories are as familiar and unchanging as the pattern of the seasons—well-known and loved stories that fit our family and the winter room like an old shoe or a well-worn work glove.

But one night Wayne does something that changes everything, and the stories stop. And in a way, it seems as though our lives stop as well. Suddenly, something is broken, and I don't know any way to fix it, or even to try to fix it. It happens the night Uncle David tells the story of the woodcutter, a story he's never told before, a story that changed forever the patterns of our lives.

MAJOR IDEAS OR THEMES

Life has patterns that help us make sense of it.

You can live with someone for years and still not know them well.

Sometimes proving something to yourself is more important than proving it to someone else.

In order to enjoy the good parts of life, we must accept the bad and ugly parts as well.

Families who work together for a common goal are more likely to be close than families whose members go their own independent ways.

BOOK REPORT IDEAS

1. In the first section of the book, the author talks about the book's needing a reader. Describe what the reader brings to this book and how each reader can make it come alive.

2. Eldon talks about the patterns of life on the farm. Compare those patterns to those you find in your own life and discuss the effect that patterns in life have on us, basing your answer on both the book and on your own experience.

3. Explain what message you think the author was trying to convey in this book. Discuss how his style of writing either clarified or hid this message.

4. What effect do you think the final scene in the book will have on Eldon and Wayne in the future, and how will it change the way they see Uncle David?

5. What did you learn from the book, and what do you think you will remember longest about it?

6. If you could ask the author one question about this book, what would it be?

BOOKTALK IDEAS

1. Focus your talk on the idea of patterns and how they shape life on the farm.

2. Write your talk in the first person, as Eldon telling about his life on the farm.

3. Try to capture the mood of the book either by quoting brief passages from it or by writing your talk in the same style that the author used.

📖 📖 📖

WITCH BABY. Francesca Lia Block. HarperCollins, 1991, 112p., $13.95. JH, HS. Eng. Quick read; realistic fiction, romance.

SUBJECT AREAS

Family relationships; Environmental concerns; Self-knowledge; Unwed mothers; Adoption; Homosexuality; Stepparents; Runaways; Racism.

CHARACTERS

Witch Baby: a girl with wild dark hair and tilted purple eyes who does not know where she belongs or who she is.

Weetzie Bat: Witch Baby's almost-mother, who tries to make people happy by being cheerful and ignoring their problems.

My Secret Agent Lover Man: Witch Baby's real father, who makes movies about what's wrong with the world.

Cherokee Bat: Weetzie's daughter, who has three fathers.

Dirk McDonald: Weetzie's best friend after My Secret Agent Lover Man, and Duck's partner for life.

Duck Drake: a surfer with a perfect blond flattop.

Valentine Jah-Love and Ping Chong: a couple who have to deal with all kinds of problems because he has dark skin and she doesn't.

Raphael Chong Jah-Love: Valentine and Ping's son. He has eyes the color of Hershey's kisses.

Coyote: My Secret Agent Lover Man's best friend. He knows how to talk to the Earth and the animals on it.

Brandy-Lynn Bat: Weetzie's mother.

Darlene Drake: Duck's mother, who learns to love her son even though he is gay.

Angel Juan: an angel who keeps reappearing in Witch Baby's dreams.

BOOKTALK

Witch Baby didn't feel like she was part of her family. She felt as though she watched them from outside, and she wasn't in any of the pictures she took of them. She wasn't like her sister, Cherokee, or like her almost-mother, Weetzie Bat, or like her father, My Secret Agent Lover Man. What was worse, everybody but her had somebody special—Weetzie and My Secret had each other, Dirk had Duck, Cherokee had Raphael, and Valentine had Ping. Only Witch Baby was alone.

She was unhappy, and so she made sure that everyone else was unhappy, too. She screamed and teased and went out of her way to do exactly what she knew would make the others miserable. She cut off Cherokee's hair. She ran away. She told Duck's mother that he was gay. She stole Coyote's special Joshua tree seeds. She took pictures of people when they were feeling and looking their worst, and in general made as much trouble as she could. The whole time she was crying inside, but she never told anyone how much she was hurting and how alone she felt.

It wasn't until she'd met the angel boy of her dreams and lost him, and until she'd gone to search for her real mother and found her, that Witch Baby began to understand that when you learn who you are, you find out where you belong, too.

Witch Baby had had her "once upon a time." Would she ever have a "happily-ever-after?"

(Adapted from a talk by Joni Richards Bodart in *Booktalk! 5.*)

MAJOR IDEAS OR THEMES

The "black sheep" in a family is usually the one who expresses the whole family's problems and pain.

There is someone special for everyone, but finding that special person can be difficult, and being with them isn't always easy.

"Who am I?" and "Where do I belong?" are two questions that every person has to answer.

Knowing who you are means knowing—and accepting—both the good and bad things about yourself.

Just because you are a black sheep doesn't mean your family doesn't love you.

It is important to do what you can to prevent bad things from happening in the world.

Homosexuality is just another way of loving someone.

BOOK REPORT IDEAS

1. Explain how Witch Baby is the black sheep in the family and give examples of the ways she shows everyone else's pain.
2. Explain why Witch Baby felt so separate from everyone else in her family.
3. Discuss the book's view of homosexuality in terms of Dirk and Duck's relationship.
4. Show how each member of the family has changed by the end of the book and explain why and how that change took place.
5. Speculate on how you think Witch Baby and her family will relate in the future.

BOOKTALK IDEAS

1. Use the language of the book to tell the story, excerpting phrases or sentences to make your talk sound like the book.
2. Write your talk from Witch Baby's point of view, using the first person.
3. Focus your talk on Witch Baby's pain and loneliness, choosing one or two scenes that particularly appeal to you to illustrate your talk.

THINNER

📖 THINNER 📖

BORN INTO LIGHT. Paul S. Jacobs. Scholastic, 1989, 149p., $2.75(pb); Scholastic, 1988, 144p., $11.95. JH, HS. Eng, Sci, Astron, Am Hist. Thoughtful; science fiction.

SUBJECT AREAS
Family relationships; Self-knowledge; Space travel; Death and dying; Aging; Love; Friendship; Science.

CHARACTERS
Roger Westwood: the narrator of the story, whose life is changed by the arrival of the "wild children."

Charlotte: Roger's older sister, who feels a special attraction to Ben, the wild boy.

Elizabeth: Roger and Charlotte's mother. She decides to take in the wild boy when the Westwoods find him near their house.

Dr. Jensen: a researcher who is investigating the phenomenon of the wild children. He eventually marries Elizabeth.

Ben: the first wild child adopted by the Westwoods.

Nell: the second wild child who comes to live with the Westwoods.

Jackson Stone: the village bully, who eventually becomes friends with Ben and Roger.

Mrs. Winfield: the village schoolteacher.

Johnny and Jim Trevalians: Ben and Roger's roommates at boarding school.

Katrina, Bobby, and Chaz: Ben and Charlotte's three children.

BOOKTALK
Roger stared in amazement at the wild boy who had appeared in the Westwoods' meadow just after dawn. The boy looked enough like him to be his twin, but he didn't know how to talk or eat—he lapped milk from a bowl like a dog. That morning there had been a big flash of light from the meadow, and after it faded away, they had seen him. Naked, scurrying across the meadow on all fours, he looked more like an animal than a person. But Roger's sister, Charlotte,

seemed to have a special rapport with him, and after she carried him into the house, their mother agreed to take him in. Not long after Ben came to live with them, Mrs. Westwood heard about another wild child, a girl, and soon Nell came to stay as well.

Who were they, the wild children who appeared throughout New England that spring of 1913? Where did they come from, and why? Why were so many of them malformed, some of them so badly that they had no chance of survival? What kind of bizarre experiment were they part of? And what would be their destiny?

MAJOR IDEAS OR THEMES
There may be populated worlds, orbiting other stars, that we know nothing about.

The most loving thing parents can do for their children may be to release them to fulfill their own destiny.

Sometimes it is better to listen to one's intuition than one's intellect.

You may have "entertained angels unawares."

Humanity has less to do with the planet we were born on than how we live our lives.

BOOK REPORT IDEAS
1. Comment on the believability of the story—given the time period in which it is set, how realistic might it be to think that wild or feral children might be refugees from another planet outside our solar system?
2. Discuss the implications this book has for our own future journeys beyond our star system.
3. Based on your view of him in the book, speculate on possible reasons Roger never married and Charlotte never remarried in an age when living alone was not as well accepted as it is now.
4. Explain why Roger chose to tell his story and to include the information in the last chapter of the book.
5. Discuss what, in your opinion, is the most important point the book is making. What part of it has the most significance for you and why?

BOOKTALK IDEAS
1. Write your talk from Ben's point of view, beginning when he first learns to speak and including his memories of how he got to Earth.
2. Focus your talk on the idea that there may be aliens among us, here for their own reasons, although we are unaware of them.

3. Focus your talk on a scene that had an emotional impact on you, for example, the milk-drinking scene in the opening pages or Nell's rescue.

📖 📖 📖

THE CAY. Theodore Taylor. Avon, 1976, 144p., $3.50(pb); Doubleday, 1987, 160p., $13.95. JH. Soc Studies, Psych. Quick read; historical fiction, adventure.

SUBJECT AREAS
Handicaps; Other countries/Caribbean; Friendship; Survival; Blacks; Racism; War; Family relationships; Aging; Death and dying.

CHARACTERS
Phillip: an 11-year-old boy who is shipwrecked on an island during World War II. An injury causes him to go blind and forces him to rely on Timothy for survival.

Timothy; an elderly black crew member who saves Phillip's life by pulling him onto the raft.

Stew: the ship's cat, which Timothy saves even though it means bad luck.

Grace Enright: Phillip's mother, who insists on making the dangerous voyage to the United States against her husband's wishes. She has taught her son to feel superior to black people.

Phillip Enright: Phillip's father, who tries to convince his wife that she and Phillip should not make the trip.

Henrik van Boven: Young Phillip's best friend.

BOOKTALK
Shipwrecked! Phillip is stranded on an island, with only an old black man and a cat for company. Worse, he is totally dependent on the old man for survival. During the shipwreck, Phillip was hit on the head, and now he is blind. Phillip's mother taught him that black people are different from white people, and what's more, that white people are better. But now Timothy is the wise one, the only one who can keep them all alive. Will Phillip continue to treat Timothy like he is a servant, or will his blindness give him the chance to see what he has never seen before?

MAJOR IDEAS OR THEMES
Skin color is not related to the kind of person someone is.

It may be impossible to understand another's profound experience—you have to have been there to know what it was really like.

A trauma or tragedy can force us to see ourselves and others in new ways.

Education is not the same as wisdom or intelligence

BOOK REPORT IDEAS
1. Describe Phillip as he is at the beginning of the book and then as he is at the end. Show how he changes and why he feels he no longer has much in common with his former friends.
2. Both Phillip and Timothy learn many things while they are on the cay. Describe some of the things they teach each other.
3. Several times Phillip describes his blindness as being an advantage. Explain in detail what you think he means by that.
4. Describe what you feel to be the most interesting or important part of this book and explain why you feel this way.

BOOKTALK IDEAS
1. Write your talk in the first person, letting Phillip tell his own story.
2. Illustrate your talk with a map of the Caribbean, showing approximately where the cay might be located.
3. Focus your talk on what it would feel like to be blind and shipwrecked with only an old man and a cat for company.
4. Write a short talk, telling only what is absolutely necessary to interest your audience—just the bare facts, without any details. This kind of talk should be no more than a few minutes long.

CLOSE ENOUGH TO TOUCH. Richard Peck. Dell, 1982, 144p., $2.95(pb.); Delacorte, 1981, 192p., $13.95. JH, HS. Eng. Quick read; realistic fiction, romance.

SUBJECT AREAS
Death and dying; Friendship; Self-knowledge; Rites of passage; School; Working.

CHARACTERS
Matt Moran: a high school junior who is devastated by the death of his girl friend, Dory.

Margaret Chasen: a high school senior who knows how to defend herself and shows Matt how to do the same.

Beth Moran: Matt's stepmother, who doesn't know how to help him deal with Dory's death.

Dad: Matt's father. Although familiar with the pain of losing a loved one, he is unable to reach out to his son.

Gram: Matt's grandmother, who works as a grocery store checker.

Ron Harvey: Matt's friend and coworker.

Ruth-Ellen Gunderson: Dory's little sister.

Mrs. Gunderson: Dory's mother. She tells Matt that he'll get over Dory's death and insists that things would never have worked out between them anyway.

Cal: the owner of Cal's Collegiate Corner, where Matt and Ron work.

Joe Hoenig: a senior and football star.

BOOKTALK
        Last summer there was Dory and "I love you's" and Fourth of July sparklers and laughter—everything he could ever want or need. But now it's a cold, bleak day in March, a day Matt knows he will remember forever—the day of Dory's funeral. He feels as though the world has ended. He doesn't know what to do or how to deal with his grief and loneliness. Crying isn't an option, getting drunk is a waste, and people are all too eager to tell him that it wouldn't have worked out anyway, or that he'll find someone else. But Matt doesn't want anyone else. He wants Dory back, Dory and all the love they'll never have.
        Months later, he still can't get Dory out of his mind. One day while he is out running, Matt sees a patch of blue in the grass next to a fence. Going closer, he sees it's a girl wearing an old-fashioned riding habit, lying still and silent in the ditch. Not far away is a horse with a saddle like no other Matt has ever seen, with horns curving out at odd angles. Who is she, and why is she dressed like someone from another century?
        The stranger turns out to be Margaret, a senior at Matt's school. Her shoulder has been dislocated in the fall. Matt takes her to the hospital emergency room and waits while her shoulder is taken care of, then he takes her home. As he is getting into bed that night, Matt realizes that he hasn't thought of Dory for hours. For the first time, he thinks that maybe she isn't the only love he'll ever have. Maybe, just maybe, the possibility of getting close to someone else is worth the risk that he might lose her and be left alone once again.
(Based on a talk by Joni Richards Bodart in *Booktalk! 2.*)

MAJOR IDEAS OR THEMES

You can't let life's losses keep you from living.

You can love more than one person during a lifetime.

You must allow yourself to grieve before you can get over the death of someone you love.

Sometimes friends will tell you things for your own good, even when you don't want to hear them.

You must let go of the past in order to move toward the future.

BOOK REPORT IDEAS

1. Matt goes through several stages in recovering from Dory's death. Trace those stages and show how other people helped him see both Dory and himself more clearly.
2. Margaret and Dory are very different in who they are, what they believe, and what their lives are like. Discuss these differences and show why Matt is attracted first to Dory. Then show how he changes so that he is attracted to Margaret.
3. Speculate on what you think will happen between Matt and Margaret and where each of them will be in five or ten years.

BOOKTALK IDEAS

1. Write your talk in the first person, letting Matt tell his own story.
2. Using a plot summary technique, lead up to Matt and Margaret's meeting.

📖 📖 📖

COWBOYS DON'T CRY. Marilyn Halvorson. Dell, 1986, 159p., $2.95(pb). JH, HS. Eng. Average; realistic fiction.

SUBJECT AREAS

Family relationships; School; Friendship; Self-knowledge; Substance abuse; Death and dying; Peer pressure.

CHARACTERS

Shane Morgan: the son of a rodeo clown and the new kid in school.

Josh Morgan: Shane's alcoholic father, who leaves the rodeo circuit after Shane inherits a small ranch from his grandfather.

Jeff Burdette: a well-known calf-roper who is one of the Morgan's best friends.

Bart Willard: the school bully who picks on Shane.

Casey Sutherland: the Morgan's pretty blond neighbor. She rescues Shane when he and Bart get into their first fist fight.

Dr. Sutherland: Casey's mother, a veterinarian who treats Angel, the Morgan's horse, after the mare gets caught in some barbed wire.

Mr. Sutherland: a lawyer who has little in common with his wife and daughter.

Cheryl Anderson: a pretty, athletic girl who wants every guy in school to chase her. To help things along, she plays Shane and Bart off against each other.

Miss Bradley: Shane's English teacher. She understands kids; they can't fool her very often.

Sheila Patterson: a social worker who thinks Shane belongs in a foster home.

BOOKTALK

Cowboys don't cry. That's what Mom used to tell me. I didn't really believe it until the night my dad lost control of the truck he was driving and she was killed in an accident. I never saw him cry, not once. After that, what I saw him do most was drink. He went from being a champion bull rider to a drunken has-been rodeo clown. We stayed on the rodeo circuit, even though he wasn't making enough money for us to live on. Then my grandfather died, and we finally got the home I'd always wanted. With my mom dead, I was his only relative, so he left me the ranch, to be held in trust by my dad until I was 18. The catch was that we had to live there—no more rodeos. I couldn't believe it when I saw my dad sign the papers, but he did, and we moved in.

I don't know why I thought he would change, why having the ranch would make a difference to him. I actually hoped he would quit drinking and remember that even if he didn't have a wife, he still had a son. But it didn't happen. He still drank, he still acted like he couldn't stand the sight of me, and he still kept going off to rodeos. So what did I do? I hung tough, telling myself that cowboys don't cry, even when they're dying inside. That spring, there were times when that's all I wanted to do—die. But that was before Casey taught me that even my mom could be wrong. Sometimes cowboys do cry.

MAJOR IDEAS OR THEMES

Sometimes the only way to solve a problem is to untangle it slowly, bit by bit.

People can't always say what they are feeling, which frequently causes misunderstandings.

Everyone needs to cry occasionally.

Running away doesn't solve problems.

Bad feelings kept inside don't fade or go away. Instead they grow and fester.

Telling the truth can sometimes get you into a fight—and sometimes it can get you out of one.

People who know how much they need each other will find a way to resolve their differences.

Just because someone else wants to fight you doesn't mean you have to agree to do it.

People don't automatically get along just because they are related. Usually they have to work at it.

Even families that seem perfect from the outside can have problems getting along.

BOOK REPORT IDEAS

1. Discuss the idea that men aren't supposed to cry, that it makes them less manly. Include your own opinions and also the views of our society on this subject.
2. Compare Shane, Casey, and Burt's families, showing how the relationships between each set of parents and between the parents and their children affected the ways these teens viewed themselves and the world around them.
3. Discuss the idea that it frequently takes a crisis to bring people who disagree together. Is this true and if so, why? Use examples from the book and from your own experiences to illustrate your comments.
4. When Bart and Shane first meet, they fight. But when Shane is in the hospital, Bart brings him the team trophy. Discuss what this gesture means in terms of how Bart regards Shane and how Shane's actions have affected him. Speculate how these two might relate to each other in the future.
5. Jeff tells Shane that he has to quit fighting his problems and concentrate on working them out a little at a time, using as an exam-

ple how Angel hurt herself more because she struggled against the barbed wire rather than just standing still and waiting for help. Explain what you think Jeff meant, using examples from the book and from your own knowledge.

BOOKTALK IDEAS

1. Focus your talk on the first scene in the book, when Josh shows up at school.
2. Start your talk with the truck accident when Shane's mother died and talk about how that has changed his life completely.
3. Write your talk from Casey's point of view as she talks about Shane and the problems that he has to deal with.
4. Write your talk from Shane's point of view, focusing on the problems he has with his dad and the anger and other emotions he is feeling.

📖 📖 📖

A DAY NO PIGS WOULD DIE. Robert Newton Peck. Dell, 1979, 139p., $3.50(pb); Knopf, 1972, 150p., $16.95. JH. Eng, Am Hist. Average; historical fiction.

SUBJECT AREAS

Family relationships; Working; Friendship; Death and dying; Self knowledge; Rites of passage.

CHARACTERS

Rob Peck: the youngest child and only son in an Amish family.

Haven Peck: Rob's father, who makes a living by killing hogs.

Lucy Peck: Rob's mother. She talks little, but loves her family deeply.

Benjamin Tanner: an affluent farmer who is the Peck's neighbor. He gives Rob a piglet as a reward for saving the life of his prize cow.

Bess Tanner: Ben Tanner's wife.

Aunt Carrie: Lucy's older sister, who lives with the Pecks.

Aunt Matty: a distant relative of Carrie and Lucy. She tends to make trouble occasionally.

Mrs. Bascome, Ira Long, Sebring and May Hillman: friends and neighbors of the Pecks.

BOOKTALK

Rob knew he shouldn't cut school, but he hated the way the other boys teased him about his Shaker clothes. As he was walking along feeling sorry for himself, he saw Mr. Tanner's cow, Apron. She was making a horrible noise, and he realized she was in big trouble. She was trying to give birth to a calf, but it was stuck, part way in and part way out. If he didn't do something quickly, Apron and the calf would both die. He tried to pull the calf out, but it was too slippery. So he took off his pants and tied one leg around the calf's neck and one leg around a tree. Then he waited for Apron to move and pull the calf out. When she didn't move, he picked up a branch and hit her and yelled until she gave a huge heave and the calf was born.

That wasn't the end of Rob's problems, though, because all of a sudden he saw that Apron wasn't breathing. There was something stuck in her throat. He stuck his hand down her throat and found something hard and round, about the size of an apple. He grabbed hold of it and pulled. But Apron had had about all she was willing to take at that point, and Rob found out the hard way that people who said cows don't bite were wrong. She almost took his arm off at the shoulder, she bit so hard. He was just lucky that Mr. Tanner found him before he bled to death. Rob was also lucky that Mr. Tanner was a generous and honorable man. He gave Rob a piglet as a reward. Rob fell in love with the little creature at first sight. But what good is a pet pig to a boy whose father makes a living butchering hogs?

MAJOR IDEAS OR THEMES

You don't need money to be rich. You can be rich in spirit, rich in family, and rich in friends.

You become an adult when you do what has to be done and do it well, no matter how painful it is for you.

People who do a job well and faithfully will be respected by those around them.

A farmer's wealth is in the land.

A farmer is a steward of the earth and its bounty.

BOOK REPORT IDEAS

1. Haven quoted the Book of Shaker to Rob. Discuss what these quotations meant to him and how they could be brought up-to-date and used as wise sayings today.

2. Rob grew from a boy to a man during the course of the book. Describe the milestones he passed along the way—the important or pivotal events in his life—and show why they were important and included in this book.
3. Describe the relationship between Haven and Rob and show how that relationship changed over time.
4. Rob learned many lessons as he grew up. Discuss which you feel is the most significant and explain why you chose it.

BOOKTALK IDEAS
1. Base your talk on the opening scene in the book, leading up to when Rob was given his pig.
2. Focus your talk on the life of the farm and the bits of Shaker wisdom Haven quoted.
3. Use a photo of a pig with a blue ribbon or a stuffed pig as a prop.

📖 📖 📖

DEAR LOVEY HART, I AM DESPERATE. Ellen Conford. Scholastic, 1977, 153p., $2.50(pb); Little, Brown, 1975, 224p., $14.95. JH. Eng, Jour. Quick read; realistic fiction, humor, romance.

SUBJECT AREAS
School; Journalism; Friendship; Psychology; Family relationships; Peer pressure.

CHARACTERS
Cassie Wasserman: a high school freshman who writes an advice column in the school newspaper under the pseudonym Lovey Hart.

Chip Custer: the editor of the school paper, who talks Cassie into becoming an advice columnist.

Marty: Cassie's close friend, and one of the students who takes Lovey Hart's advice.

Terry: one of Cassie's two best girlfriends. She has a crush on her French teacher.

Claudia: Cassie's other best friend. She has never been in love until she discovers Chip.

Jennifer: Cassie's nosy younger sister.

Mr. and Mrs. Wasserman: Cassie's parents. Mr. Wasserman is a guidance counselor at Cassie's high school.

Mr. Gross: the faculty advisor for the student paper.

BOOKTALK
It was both the greatest and the worst year of my life—my year as Lovey Hart, advice columnist for the school newspaper. I never would have done it if Chip, the editor, wasn't such a hunk. But he's so gorgeous I let him talk me into it. At first it was fun, and everybody loved Lovey Hart. I could do no wrong. Then it all changed, and I started getting angry letters from kids who didn't like what I'd written. Some people thought I was flippant and didn't take their problems seriously enough. Others didn't like the serious advice I'd given them. I wanted out, but Chip said the column was too popular, and he wouldn't let me quit.

I began to wonder. What would happen if everyone found out who Lovey Hart really was? Even my best friends were mad at her. But where does an advice columnist go for advice?

MAJOR IDEAS OR THEMES
No one has all the answers.

A person's problems are serious to that person, even if they seem silly to someone else.

Some people may ask for advice when they don't really want to hear it.

Liars frequently, if not always, get caught.

Friendship includes forgiveness.

A flippant remark can sound clever to the person who says it, but cruel and uncaring to the person at whom it is directed.

BOOK REPORT IDEAS
1. Write your book report as if it were a letter to Lovey Hart and her reply.
2. Write your report as if it were a news story in your local school paper.
3. Discuss the place of advice columnists in our society today and the function they serve. Compare Lovey's advice to some of the responses you have seen recently in your local newspapers.

4. Analyze and compare the positive and negative responses that Lovey got. Show why people responded either positively or negatively and whether they really wanted to be helped.
5. Discuss the choices that Cassie made, first her decision to be Lovey Hart and then how she handled the job and dealt with her friends' and family's disapproval of Lovey. Choices sometimes eventually lock us into one way of responding or acting. Decide whether this happened to Cassie and support your stand with quotes from the book.
6. People respond to the advice they hear, which may not be the advice that they are given. Show how people misinterpreted the advice Lovey gave them and how that affected their response to it.

BOOKTALK IDEAS
1. Write your talk as if it were a letter to Lovey and her reply.
2. Use quotes from some of the letters to build the body of your talk.
3. Center your talk around the problems the characters in the book have, building up to the problem Carrie has with Lovey Hart.

DEVIL'S RACE. Avi. Avon, 1987, 128p., $2.75(pb); Harper & Row, 1984, 160p., $12.95. JH. Eng, Am Hist. Quick read; supernatural.

SUBJECT AREAS
Family relationships; Ghosts; Self-knowledge; School.

CHARACTERS
John Proud: a tall, lanky 16-year-old.

John Proud: the great-great-great-great-grandfather of the present-day John Proud. He was hanged as a demon in 1854.

Uncle Dave: the older brother of the current John Proud's father.

Nora Fenton: John and Dave's cousin. She lives near the cemetery where the first John Proud is buried.

Tom Fenton: Nora's husband.

Ann Fenton: Nora and Tom's daughter. She is about John's age.

Martin Fenton: Ann's younger brother.

BOOKTALK

When John Proud first heard about his great-great-great-great-grandfather, who had been hanged as a demon in 1854, he was intrigued. Later, when his uncle offered to take him to visit his cousins and to see his ancestor's grave, he felt strangely compelled to go. They were within a few hundred yards of the cemetery when Uncle Dave got sick and said they had to go back, that the trip had been a mistake. But John felt the same sense of urgency that had come over him when the trip was first proposed. He knew, without knowing why, that he couldn't leave without seeing the grave, so he went on alone.

There was nothing unusual about the grave itself—just an old, mossy tombstone. But the tall, lanky teenager seated on top of it looked strangely familiar. "Hello, John," said the boy. "I'm John Proud, the first John Proud. I'm delighted to meet you." Suddenly John realized why he looked so familiar. The boy could have been his twin—looking at him was like looking in a mirror.

John soon realized, however, that his double represented a deadly threat—he wanted to take over John's life, his body, his very soul. And although his ancestor said he'd never take anything that John didn't want to give him, John knew that he was lying, and that he was in terrible danger from this boy who looked so sane, so normal, and so much like himself.

MAJOR IDEAS OR THEMES

Sometimes what seems "right" is exactly the opposite of what you really need to do.

Evil from the past can come alive in the present with the help of a human partner.

Love can conquer evil.

Be true to the best in yourself.

BOOK REPORT IDEAS

1. Discuss whether the first John Proud is just a figment of the current John's imagination. How can our imaginations control our actions?
2. Look at the ways the two Johns are alike and different.
3. John believes that after he sees his ancestor, his thoughts—and only his thoughts—can change reality. Take a stance either for or against this statement and defend your position using quotes from the book and your own ideas.
4. Discuss the nature of good and evil as seen in various characters in the book, looking at those who are either all good or all bad and at those who are a mixture of the two.

5. This book is fiction, but the author has done several things to make the people and action in it believable. Discuss whether the situation, the action, and the characters seem realistic or unrealistic.

BOOKTALK IDEAS
1. Present your talk in the first person, taking the character of one of the two Johns and telling the story from that perspective.
2. Center your talk on the first time the two Johns meet or on the dichotomy of good and evil that they represent.
3. Focus on the way the current John believes he is being taken over by his ancestor. If you give the talk in the first person, show this in what he says and how he says it. Give your audience a taste of what it might be like to be invaded by an evil spirit.
4. Use the newspaper clipping about the first John's death as part of your talk.

📖 📖 📖

DOUBLE TROUBLE. Barthe DeClements. Scholastic, 1988, 144p., $2.75(pb); Viking, 1987, 168p., $12.95. JH, HS. Eng, Psych. Quick read; supernatural, suspense, mystery.

SUBJECT AREAS
Parapsychology; Adoption; Family relationships; Death and dying; Child abuse; Religion; Religious persecution; Friendship; Love.

CHARACTERS
Phillip and Faith: twins who are separated after their parents and older sister Madalyn, are killed in a car accident. They communicate with each other through letters and extrasensory perception. Faith is telepathic, and Phillip uses astral projection to "travel" outside his body.

Sue Ellen: a friend of Faith. She has a crush on Mr. Gessert, a teacher.

Mr. Gessert: a history teacher whom Faith mistrusts.

Howard and Cynthia Wangsley: Phillip's foster parents. They try to force him to adopt their narrow standards of behavior and punish him when he refuses to cooperate.

Aunt Linda: the twin sister of Phillip and Faith's mother. She agrees to keep Faith after the accident, but gives her little financial or emotional support.

Roxanne: a loyal friend of Phillip.

Jake: a student in Mr. Gessert's class and Faith's friend. He listens to her concerns about the teacher.

Roger Clinton: Madalyn's boyfriend, an underwater archaeologist who uses psychic means to try to locate shipwrecks.

Mrs. Thompson: a teacher whom Faith and other students feel they can trust.

BOOKTALK
As soon as Faith centered herself and thought about her twin brother, she knew that Phillip had been moved to a foster home. But she didn't know that he was moving into one of the most dangerous situations he'd ever been in anymore than she knew that one of her teachers was threatening her very life.

The twins had always been able to communicate telepathically and through astral projection. Now when their lives are in danger, these powers may be the only things that can save them.

Perhaps you've laughed at the idea of reading someone else's mind or being in two places at once—but before you say it couldn't possibly happen, find out what these twins have to say about it and how their powers helped them save their lives.

MAJOR IDEAS OR THEMES
Twins often have special connections with one another.

No one should try to force their religious beliefs on another person.

Peace and love can sometimes overcome hatred and evil.

It is best to forget past jealousies lest they poison your present happiness.

It is important to believe in and stand up for yourself.

Everyone needs the love and support of others—if not family, then friends.

Friends support one another when doing so is difficult.

BOOK REPORT IDEAS
1. Examine the questions of religious freedom and religious persecution as they are presented in the book.
2. Compare the twins' ethical standards to those of the other characters in the book, especially those of the Wangsleys and the cult they belonged to.

3. Discuss in some detail what you consider to be the most interesting part of the book and explain why you chose that part.
4. There are a number of obvious and underlying ethical questions in the book. Explain what they are and show how various characters justified their beliefs and actions.
5. Various kinds of psychic phenomena are presented in the book. Discuss your opinion on whether they might be real and if so, the implications that this has for you and our society in general.

BOOKTALK IDEAS
1. Use quotes from the twins' letters as your booktalk.
2. Tell the story in the first person from either Faith's or Phillip's point of view.
3. Center your talk around the question of psychic phenomena and whether they are real.

HAROLD AND MAUDE. Colin Higgins. Avon, 1979, 145p., $3.50(pb). HS. Eng, Art. Quick read; romance, humor.

SUBJECT AREAS
Aging; Death and dying; Suicide; Family relationships; Self-knowledge.

CHARACTERS
Harold Chasen: an 18-year-old who is in love with death.

Maude: Countess Matilda Chardin, who is 79 years old and in love with life.

Mrs. Chasen: Harold's mother, who has many plans for him.

Victor E. Ball: Harold's uncle, the brigadier general.

Dr. Harley: Harold's psychiatrist, who doesn't understand him at all.

BOOKTALK
Harold is 18 and in love with death. Maude is 79 and in love with life. Harold is making a career out of committing suicide (he's done it more than 15 times so far) because, as he says, "I enjoy being dead." Maude spends her time looking for new experiences and enjoying being alive. They do have one thing in common: They both like to go to funerals. Maude goes because funerals are about change, and she thinks they're fun. Harold goes because he likes the feeling of being

close to death. They meet after a funeral when Maude uses her set of skeleton keys to steal Harold's hearse—and then offers him a ride home. That's the beginning of an unusual love affair between the oddest of odd couples. Harold is fascinated by Maude's freedom, her energy, and her intense love of life—all things he has never experienced. He isn't able to teach her much about death, but she teaches him quite a bit about life. Meanwhile, his mother has decided that marriage is just the thing to distract him from suicide. Harold is agreeable, but he doesn't want to marry any of the girls his mother has arranged for him to meet. He wants to marry Maude! Join Harold and Maude on their wild and wacky adventure, and discover what life, love, and death can really mean. Their story is strange, funny, and wonderful—and one you'll never forget.

(Based on a talk by Joni Richards Bodart in *Booktalk! 3*.)

MAJOR IDEAS OR THEMES

Life is full of changes, of which death is only one.

Build bridges, not walls.

Every person is unique. No one like you has ever existed before or will ever exist again.

Don't get attached to things, because life is transitory.

Take charge of your life, don't let it take charge of you.

It is up to each of us to decide whether to enjoy life or to suffer through it.

"Live, live, live! Life is a banquet and most poor fools are starving to death!"—Patrick Dennis, *Auntie Mame*.

BOOK REPORT IDEAS

1. Discuss: We are all, in some way, Harolds trying to become Maudes.
2. Maude told Harold bits and pieces of her life. Putting those pieces together, write a biography of Maude, showing how her experiences made her the person she is in the book.
3. Speculate on what you think happens after the end of the book. Who will Harold be at 30, at 50, at 79, and what will his life be like? Compare this to the person Harold might have become had he never met Maude.
4. Discuss what Maude believed was important and what the rules were by which she lived her life.
5. This book is written in a "cinematic style," in that the reader can easily see a "movie" of what is happening when reading the book. In addition, the movie of the book uses not only the same scenes

but also most of the dialogue. Give examples of how the author produced this effect.

BOOKTALK IDEAS
1. Write the talk from Harold's point of view, using his own words to show how he changed during the course of the book, leading up to his decision to marry Maude.
2. Focus your talk on the bits of wisdom that Maude shares with Harold to help you tell their story.
3. Center your talk around one or two scenes or incidents between Harold and Maude.

📖 📖 📖

HEARTBEAT. Norma Fox Mazer and Harry Mazer. Bantam, 1989, 165p., $13.95. HS. Eng, Psych. Thoughtful; realistic fiction, romance.

SUBJECT AREAS
Death and dying; Friendship; Ethics; Self-knowledge; Working.

CHARACTERS
Todd Ellerbee: a tall, intelligent, blond 17-year-old who is still afraid of girls.

Amos Vaccaro: a friend of Todd, who saved him from drowning and now wants a favor.

Hilary Goodman: a girl at Todd's school who has her eye on Todd.

Bob Ellerbee: Todd's father, a restless man who is usually distant from his son.

Loretta: Todd's boss at the bowling alley and his father's girlfriend.

Jen Kopp: a junior high school girl and a member of the Todd Ellerbee Fan Club.

Amy Vaccaro: Amos's twin sister.

Mr. and Mrs. Vaccaro: Amos and Amy's parents.

Scott: Loretta's son.

BOOKTALK

Amos was the reason Todd's heart was still beating. He was still choking and spitting up water when he told Amos, "Anything you want, ever, I'm your man."

It had been four years since Amos had pulled Todd from the lake, and in all that time he had never asked for anything—until now. He wanted Todd to introduce him to Hilary, who went to Todd's school. It seemed a simple enough request, but Todd still had trouble talking to girls, even if he was 17, tall, and good-looking. By the time he managed to get Amos's message across to Hilary, he was beginning to realize that he was in love with her himself, and she loved him. Now what were they going to do?

What do love and loyalty mean when you're caught in a three-way trap? Can a heart keep on beating after it's broken? And how many hearts will stop beating before the situation is finally resolved? (Based on a talk by Jeff Blair in *Booktalk! 4.*)

MAJOR IDEAS OR THEMES

You can't choose whether to fall in love or who you fall in love with

Sometimes friendship is more important than romantic love.

The impending death of a friend makes all other considerations secondary.

Looks can be deceiving.

Even people who seem to "have it all" probably don't.

Death and illness are neither logical nor fair.

When something is inevitable, quit struggling and face it with grace and dignity.

BOOK REPORT IDEAS

1. Discuss the relationship between Todd and his father and the impact that it made on the rest of Todd's life.
2. Examine the question of obligation in friendship, looking at whether Todd was truly obligated to Amos because Amos saved his life.
3. Explain the qualities in Todd and Hilary that attracted them to each other.
4. Discuss the reasons Todd decides to visit his grandparents.
5. Speculate on what you think will happen when Todd returns home from England. Will he and Hilary be able to reestablish their relationship, or will one or both of them have changed too much?

And if they have changed, describe what those changes might be and give your rationale for them.

6. Discuss Amos's character and his relationship with Todd and Hilary. Giving examples from the book, explain how he showed his friendship for each of them.

7. There are other situations in literature and history similar to the one in this book: The go-between also falls in love with the friend's beloved. Compare this book with one or more of those other instances.

BOOKTALK IDEAS

1. Using the first person in each case, let Todd, Hilary, and Amos talk about each other and the triangle they form. Remember, they have very different views of the situation. Be sure what they say is true to their characters.

2. Base your talk on the idea of obligation between friends and whether Todd is really obligated to give up Hilary because Amos saved his life. This talk could start with Todd remembering when Amos saved him and could then continue with his questioning the incident's effect on his life now.

3. Let Hilary tell the story, keeping in mind that at first she doesn't know the complete story of why Todd is interested in her. Show how she falls in love with him, and then hint at her love for Amos and the quandary it puts her in.

📖 📖 📖

I HEARD THE OWL CALL MY NAME. Margaret Craven. Dell, 1980, 159p., $3.95(pb). HS. Eng, Soc Studies. Thoughtful; realistic fiction, adventure.

SUBJECT AREAS
Religion; Death and dying; Self-knowledge; Friendship; Native Americans; Love; Other countries/Canada.

CHARACTERS
Mark Brian: a young vicar who is sent to spend his last days at Kingcome

The Bishop: the church official who assigns Mark to the Indian villages around Kingcome.

Caleb: an old canon who tells Mark about the Indians he will live with.

Jim Wallace: the first Indian Mark meets. He takes Mark to the village.

Chief Eddy: the tribal chief.

T. P. Wallace: the tribe's orator.

Marta Stephens: one of the grandmothers of the tribe.

Gordon: a young Indian who attends the government school at Alert Bay.

Keetah: one of the young girls of the village. She is to marry Gordon when he returns.

Mrs. Hudson: the tribal matriarch and Keetah's great-grandmother.

Peter: the old carver for the village.

BOOKTALK

The doctor said to the bishop, "So you see, my lord, Mark Brian can live no more than three years and doesn't know it. Will you tell him, and what will you do with him?"

The bishop said to the doctor, "Yes, I'll tell him, but not yet. If I tell him now, he'll try too hard. How much time has he for an active life?"

"A little less than two years if he's lucky."

"So short a time to learn so much? It leaves me no choice. I shall send him to my hardest parish. I shall send him to Kingcome on patrol of the Indian villages."

"Then I hope you'll pray for him, my lord."

But the bishop only answered gently that it was where he would wish to go if he were young again and in Mark Brian's place.

Mark believes that he is going to the Indian village of Kingcome to guide and help the people there. But in reality, they will be his guides and teachers, as he learns what will be the most important lesson of his life—he must learn enough about the meaning of life to know how to die, and he must learn it all too soon.

MAJOR IDEAS OR THEMES

When you show respect for others and their way of life, they will learn to respect you in turn.

One should always look, listen, and think before speaking.

The meaning of life is simple, not complex.

Sometimes the best way to help someone is to show them their strengths, not support their weaknesses.

Death is an essential part of life.

You cannot force friendship, you can only create the space for it to happen.

When life is a daily struggle to survive, the truth becomes very clear and very simple.

BOOK REPORT IDEAS
1. Discuss in detail what you would have wanted your bishop to do if you had been in Mark's place.
2. List some of the lessons that Mark learned and from whom he learned them.
3. Speculate how you think Mark will be remembered in Kingcome and how the villagers will describe him to his successor.
4. The bishop wanted Mark to learn the meaning of life. Explain what you understand to be the meaning of life, first from the book and then from your own experiences.
5. Sometimes books that are very moving are also very painful to read or to think about afterward. Explain why you think the author wrote this book and which part or parts of it were most meaningful to you and why.
6. One of the themes in this book is learning to live in another culture. Discuss some of the things you learned about how to do this and how you might apply them in your own life.

BOOKTALK IDEAS
1. Write your talk in the first person as if you were the bishop.
2. Write your talk as if you were Mark, speaking in the first person.
3. Start your talk with Mark's arrival at Kingcome and then do a character description talk as you introduce some of the villagers that became special or important to Mark.
4. Focus your talk upon the mood of the book, stressing the way the villagers thought and felt and the way Mark responded to the land and its people.
5. Focus your talk on some of the bits of philosophy that Mark learned or on some of the Indian legends included in the book.

IF I ASKED YOU, WOULD YOU STAY? Eve Bunting. Harper & Row, 1987, 160p., $2.75(pb); Harper & Row, 1984, 160p., $12.89. HS. Eng. Thoughtful; realistic fiction, romance.

SUBJECT AREAS
Runaways; Friendship; Self-knowledge; Orphans.

CHARACTERS

Charles Robert O'Neill (Crow): an orphan who finds a home in a secret place above a carousel.

Valentine Love: a girl whom Crow saves from drowning.

Ethan: Crow's friend, who runs the carousel on weekends.

Bruce: the owner of Bruce's sporting goods shop, where Crow works.

Robbie Johnson: another boy who works at Bruce's.

Kim Manilea: a girl who works at Bruce's. She has a crush on Crow.

Marty: a man whom Valentine fears.

BOOKTALK

He is the Crow, and the Crow always flies alone, with nothing and no one to hold him back.

Since leaving the orphanage, Crow has lived in a series of foster homes. Finally, in a southern California beach town, he finds his first real home—a secret apartment hidden behind a sliding wall, above the carousel where he worked all summer. Now it's fall, the carousel is silent, and he has a job in a sporting goods store.

Late one night, Crow sees someone swimming away from shore. It looks as though he intends to go on and on, until he sinks out of sight forever. Crow runs downstairs to where the dinghy is kept and rows out to the rescue. But when he pulls the swimmer into the boat, he discovers that it is a girl. Crow takes her home to his secret place and offers to let her stay with him a few days, even though it means he will lose his precious privacy. The girl's name is Valentine. She's a runaway and as scared of commitment as Crow is. Gradually, though, they become friends and start to trust each other.

But their pasts are catching up with them. Now they must find a way not only to deal with the past, but to survive what is happening to them in the present. Can they find a way out together, or will the Crow fly on alone, never finding a roost to come home to?
(Adapted from a talk by Judy Druse in *Booktalk! 3*.)

MAJOR IDEAS OR THEMES

Shutting everyone else out of your life may make you feel safer, but it will also make you lonely.

You can't run away from your past, because sooner or later it will catch up with you.

It is better to face your problems than to run away from them.

Trusting means taking a chance, but it is frequently worth the risk.

Reaching out to others means that they can also reach out to you.

Your faith in yourself, not solitude, is what keeps you safe.

BOOK REPORT IDEAS
1. Compare Crow at the beginning and end of the book. Look at how he changed and why.
2. Compare Valentine when Crow rescued her and at the end of the book. Look at how she changed and why.
3. There are a number of ethical questions in this book, such as: Was it right or wrong for Crow to take over Sasha's secret apartment, especially after her death? Was it right or wrong for Valentine and Crow to hide what had really happened when Marty died? Was it right or wrong for Valentine to run away from her mother and stepfather? Discuss your responses to one or more of these questions or to other ethical dilemmas you see in the book. Be sure to support your position with not only quotes from the book, but also with your own beliefs and ethical convictions.
4. Crow wants to keep Sasha's room a secret even after the building is destroyed. This is a romantic, but not a very practical, notion, because destroying the building will reveal not only the secret apartment but also all of Sasha's things. Discuss what you would do if you were Crow, realizing that you don't want to see her things strewn where anyone can see them and that if you do nothing, that will be inevitable. How would you maintain both your own and her privacy?

BOOKTALK IDEAS
1. Focus your talk on the inner conflict Crow feels about letting Valentine become a part of his life. This would probably work best in the first person, as if Crow were speaking.
2. Write your talk as if it were a dialogue between Crow and Valentine, either using bits of conversation from the book or making up a conversation that they might have had but didn't.
3. Describe the scene when Crow rescues Valentine and discovers she is a girl.

📖 📖 📖

THE INCREDIBLE JOURNEY. Sheila Burnford. Bantam, 1977, 145p., $2.95(pb); Amereon, 1961, 145p., $13.95. JH, HS. Eng, Soc Studies. Quick read; adventure, suspense.

SUBJECT AREAS
Animals; Survival; Friendship; Travel; Love.

CHARACTERS
Tao: a clever Siamese who does not believe he is a cat.

Bodger: an old bull terrier with a wicked sense of humor.

Luath: a young Labrador retriever, to whom nothing is as important as being back with his master.

John Longridge: a writer and bachelor who volunteers to look after the three animals for several months while their family is in England.

Mrs. Oakes and Bert Oakes: a couple who look after Longridge and his house.

Jim Hunter: Longridge's good friend and Luath's owner. He is a professor in a small town more than 200 miles from Longridge's cabin.

Elizabeth Hunter: Longridge's daughter and Tao's owner.

Peter Hunter: Bodger's owner for most of the dog's life.

Members of an Ojibwa tribe, Old Mr. Aubyn, Rieno Nurmi, Mrs. Nurmi, Helvi Nurmi, James and Nell Mackenzie: kind and caring people who help the three travelers in various ways.

BOOKTALK
It was fall, and the three travelers were enjoying the Indian summer as they began their journey. Their leader, Luath, was determined to get home as soon as possible. It was he that persuaded the other two, Tao and Bodger, to come with him They missed their old home, but without Luath's urging, they would have been content to wait and see what the future brought.

Once on the road, the three companions had to deal with situations and problems they had never before imagined. They faced down an angry bear intent on protecting her cub. They made friends with a tribe of Ojibwa, and they made an enemy of a farmer whose chicken they tried to steal for supper. A little girl rescued Tao from drowning, and a kindly farmer helped Luath get the porcupine quills out of his face. Everywhere they went, people remembered them, talked about them, and wished them well on their journey.

These were no ordinary travelers. Luath was a young Labrador retriever, Bodger, an elderly bull terrier, and Tao, a Siamese cat. Their goal would have challenged experienced human travelers, and it seemed an impossible feat for three animals who had always depended on humans to take care of them. Would they survive 200 miles of Canadian wilderness and reach the home they missed so badly?

MAJOR IDEAS OR THEMES
Friends defend each other.

Even animals have ways of repaying those who help them.

Friendship and love between animals can run as deep and as strong as they do between humans.

Determination can find a way against the most incredible odds.

Many animals are steadfastly loyal to the humans they consider to be "their people."

Many animals have the intelligence to be able to solve problems and to learn.

BOOK REPORT IDEAS
1. Use a map of Canada to illustrate your report, showing the route the three animals took and noting on it where each of their adventures took place.
2. Discuss the idea of friendship as seen in the relationship among the animals and compare it to the relationships among human friends, showing some of the similarities and some of the differences.
3. The bond between dog and master is the cause of the long journey. Discuss the connection between pets and their owners or masters. Show how this bond can change people's lives and how severing that bond can cause the same kind of loss and depression that a human death can.
4. Each of the animals has his own distinct personality. Show how the author accomplished this and discuss the dominant quality of each one's personality.

BOOKTALK IDEAS
1. Write the talk in the first person, speaking as one of the animals. Remember to include only what that animal could know about or perceive.
2. Focus on the character of each animal, giving short sketches of each from a variety of points of view as people met them along their journey. In other words, show how differently people saw them.
3. Focus your talk on one or two incidents in the book where one or more of the animals were in danger, leading up to the climax of the scene but not giving away the resolution.

4. Summarize the plot up to the point when they left on their journey and end the talk by referring to several of the dangers they would have to face.

A KINDNESS. Cynthia Rylant. Orchard/Watts, 1988, 128p., $13.95. JH, HS. Eng, Psych. Quick read; realistic fiction.

SUBJECT AREAS
Family relationships; Self-knowledge; Unwed mothers.

CHARACTERS
Chip Becker: the 18-year-old son of an artist mother and an absent father.

Anne Becker: Chip's mother. She is wise and determined.

Benjamin George: the New York City art dealer who sells Anne's work.

Jeannie Perlman: Chip's girlfriend.

Randy: a good friend of Chip and Anne.

Dusky Anne Becker: Chip's new baby sister.

BOOKTALK
Chip and his mother had lived alone for 15 years, ever since his father moved to Australia. They were alike in ways they were not even aware of, and part of each other's lives in ways that would have been impossible had there been brothers or sisters or husbands with them. They were a family, and their relationship was more intense because there were only two of them. Chip was the practical one; Anne was an artist and her paintings supported them. Once a year she went to New York to take her paintings to her dealer, who sold them for her. Chip was in the tenth grade and in love with Jeannie Perlman and wanted to marry her someday. But when Anne told him what had happened, their lives changed forever. She was pregnant and planned to keep the baby. But she refused to tell Chip who the father was. She said it was her business, not his. It was her life—but because it was Chip's life too, no matter what she said, he looked for someone to blame and he chose the baby's father. What he didn't realize was that in looking so hard for a man to hate, he would risk losing the two women he loved most in the world, Jeannie and Anne. Is finding out who Dusky's father is worth risking that much?

MAJOR IDEAS OR THEMES

You can love other people, but you can never own them.

Holding too tightly to people can drive them away.

Sometimes what is right for someone else is wrong for you.

Loving someone means being able to let them go.

BOOK REPORT IDEAS

1. Show how Chip changed over the course of the year that the book covers.
2. Show how Chip, Anne, Randy, Jeannie, and Ben demonstrate the main idea, "Love is letting go."
3. Discuss what Chip did to lead Jeannie to break up with him and what he could have done differently that would have prevented it.
4. Discuss the confrontation between Chip and Ben and what you think would have happened if that conversation had never taken place.
5. Explain why Anne decided to find a new dealer for her paintings.

BOOKTALK IDEAS

1. Tell the story in the first person from Chip's perspective.
2. Use the section of the story in italics or boldface type as a focus for your talk.
3. Create the mood of the book in your booktalk by using quotes of sentences or scenes to build your talk.
4. Use the relationship between Chip and Anne as the focus of your talk, describing how it always was, leading up to the scene when Anne tells Chip she is pregnant and he realizes that their old relationship is gone forever.

📖 📖 📖

THE LEAVING. Lynn Hall. Macmillan, 1988, 128p., $2.95(pb); Macmillan, 1980, 128p., $11.95. JH, HS. Eng, Home Ec, Psych. Quick read; realistic fiction.

SUBJECT AREAS

Family relationships; Friendship; Rites of passage; Working; Self-knowledge.

CHARACTERS

Roxanne Armstrong: a high school graduate who leaves her beloved family farm to prove that she can make it on her own in the city.

Thora Armstrong: Roxanne's mother, who finds it hard to express her feelings. She is suffering the consequences of decisions she made when she was younger.

Cletus Armstrong: Roxanne's father. Nothing in his life has turned out the way he expected, but now he has a chance to start over.

Norma Zimmerman: one of Roxanne's best friends, a fellow basketball player and artist.

Alene Taylor: Roxanne's other best friend. She also plays basketball.

BOOKTALK

Roxanne loved the farm. She'd lived there all her life and she knew she'd always be happy there. Still, she felt that she had to prove to herself that she could survive if she left. It had been more than a year since high school graduation. The haying was done, the corn was in. It was time for her to go. She chose Des Moines, the largest city in the state, as her destination. She knew that if she could survive there, she could survive anywhere.

Thora, Roxanne's mother, loved the farm as much as her daughter did. She had been born there and had left only once. Now she was determined never to leave again.

Cletus, Roxanne's father, hated the farm. He felt trapped there and wanted more than anything else to escape. Very little about his life had turned out the way he'd wanted it to, and he wanted a second chance.

Everything that we do affects someone else to some extent. Even a small action can lead to dramatic changes, just as a touch can topple a house of cards. Roxanne's decision, even though she made it for herself alone, set in motion a chain of events that would change their lives forever.

MAJOR IDEAS OR THEMES

Life doesn't always turn out the way we expect it to.

We have to live with the consequences of the decisions we made in the past.

If you don't share your feelings with others, they may come to the wrong conclusions about you.

Life doesn't have to be exciting or dramatic to be happy and fulfilling.

Each person must find his or her own path to happiness and fulfillment.

Proving something to yourself is more important than proving it to anyone else.

BOOK REPORT IDEAS
1. Compare Thora and Cletus's expectations with those of their daughter, showing which were realistic and which were not and why.
2. Speculate on what Thora and Roxanne will be like five or ten years from the end of the book and explain your rationale for the direction you predict for their lives.
3. This book is written from three different points of view. Discuss how this technique changes the reader's perception of each of the three main characters.
4. Explain why Roxanne needed to leave home when she loved the farm so much, what she learned before she returned, and why she felt that she could return when she did.
5. Based on your understanding of the three main characters, discuss whether more and better communication among them would have ultimately made a difference in the way the book ended. Be sure to include in your discussion citations from the book that support your arguments.
6. All families have certain unwritten rules that govern the way family members interact with each other. Explain what the rules in the Armstrong family were and how they had developed over time.

BOOKTALK IDEAS
1. Using quotes from each of the main characters, show how each one's hidden expectations led to their final confrontation. This talk could be done in either the first or third person.
2. Focus your talk on the idea of change and how a whole family can be changed by one member's decision or action.
3. Focus your talk on the idea of secrets and the secrets that each of the family members kept from the other two.

LEROY AND THE OLD MAN. W. E. Butterworth. Scholastic, 1987, 168p., $2.50(pb). HS. Eng, Sociology, Psych. Quick read; realistic fiction.

SUBJECT AREAS
Blacks; Crime and delinquency; Family relationships; Working; Self-knowledge; Rites of passage; Friendship; Grandparents; Peer pressure.

CHARACTERS
Leroy Chambers: the unwilling witness to a murder committed by the Wolves, one of the most dangerous gangs in Chicago.

Mrs. Chambers: Leroy's mother, who persuades him to go live with his grandfather until things cool down.

Aaron Chambers: Leroy's grandfather, a Mississippi shrimper who teaches Leroy some things about work and a great deal about people.

Elton Davidson, Howard Pettaway, and B. J. Norton: gang members who attack Mrs. Carson and warn Leroy not to talk to the police.

Moriarity: a white undercover cop who looks like a junkie. He works in the projects where Leroy lives.

Paul Davis: a Chicago housing authority police officer who puts pressure on Leroy to testify against the Wolves.

Mr. Alfred: the owner and chef of a New Orleans restaurant that buys Aaron's shrimp. He is also Aaron's friend.

Sheriff Greenhow: the local sheriff, another of Aaron's friends.

Joe Keller: the owner and chef at Le Cruset, one of the best restaurants in New Orleans, and a friend of Aaron and Leroy.

Leroy's father: a man who deserted his wife and son when Leroy was 12. He reappears when he finds out that Leroy is in trouble with the Wolves.

BOOKTALK

What would you do if you were a witness to a murder committed by three members of one of the most dangerous gangs around? Staying in town would be hazardous to your health. The only way you know you'll be safe is to get out of town and go some place where they'll never find you. That's what Leroy does. He leaves Chicago and goes to stay with his grandfather in Mississippi.

His grandfather isn't anything like what Leroy expected. He's a shrimper, independent, stubborn, and sure he's right, even when Leroy knows he isn't. He just doesn't understand that even though the three gang members Leroy saw are in jail, the other members are still out there, looking for Leroy. He is right about some things, though, like people, and working, and the real meaning of respect. Then, just about the time Leroy decides that he likes the way his life is going, the Chicago police show up at his grandfather's house. They tell him that he's a material witness, and they make it clear that if he doesn't show up for the trial, or if he develops amnesia on the witness stand, he'll regret it.

What is Leroy supposed to do? No matter what he decides, he'll be in trouble with someone. He can keep running, and maybe escape the Wolves, or he can testify, hope that the police can keep him alive, and make his grandfather proud of him. But he can't help but wonder—just how proud will the old man be if Leroy is the next person the Wolves decide doesn't deserve to live?

MAJOR IDEAS OR THEMES

No one else can tell you what's right for you, you have to decide that for yourself.

Sometimes doing the right thing will put you in danger.
It's easier to believe in yourself if someone you trust believes in you first.

Some mistakes are so major and longlasting that they can be neither forgiven nor forgotten.

If you don't respect yourself, no one else will respect you either.

Having money doesn't mean much if you don't also have the respect of others.

True courage is being afraid and doing what needs to be done anyway.

It's better to examine the consequences of a decision before you make it than to discover them afterward.

BOOK REPORT IDEAS

1. Leroy describes his grandfather as someone who thinks in black and white. Give several examples that illustrate this and discuss what some of the reasons might be for his having this philosophy or trait.
2. In the beginning of this book, Leroy is willing for other people to make the decisions that shape his life. By the end, he has decided to make his own decisions. Show how this change took place and when he first decided to do what he felt was right, not what someone else said was right.
3. Discuss the idea of friendship as it is seen in the book, including how to make a friend, how to keep one, and the value of friendship.
4. Examine the idea of bravery, what it is and what it means. You might want to examine in your discussion the quote from Shakespeare: "Cowards die many times before their deatHS. but the valiant never taste of death but once." Also include your own idea of what you would have done in Leroy's situation, based on your own philosophy and experiences.
5. Discuss the different views of racism that Leroy saw in the North and in the South, and explain why you think those differences existed.

BOOKTALK IDEAS
1. Write your talk in the first person as Leroy tells his story.
2. Focus your talk on the idea of gang violence and how it affects even innocent bystanders.
3. Write a plot summary talk, leading up to one of the suspenseful climaxes in the book.
4. Use a newspaper clipping that resembles the story Leroy sees in the paper to illustrate your talk.

THE MONUMENT. Gary Paulsen. Delacorte, 1991, 149p., $15.00. JH. Eng, Am Hist, Art. Quick read; realistic fiction.

SUBJECT AREAS
Self-knowledge; Handicaps; Adoption; Friendship; Art; Animals.

CHARACTERS
Rocky Turner: a 13-year-old loner with a crippled leg.

Emma and Fred Hemesvedt: Rocky's adoptive parents. Although they are kind to her, they are always drunk by 9:00 AM, so she is left pretty much on her own.

Python: Rocky's dog, who is her best friend and constant companion.

Mick: an artist who comes to town to design a war monument.

Mrs. Langdon: the woman who hires Mick to design the monument.

BOOKTALK
It was a quiet, dusty little Kansas town until the morning Mick arrived. After that everything changed, and nothing has been the same since. My name is Rocky, and I live in Bolton, Kansas. My best friend is my dog, Python. I really think I didn't have any other friends until Mick came and showed me what art really is, and how to look at people and see what's really inside them.

But this story isn't about me—it's about Mick, and how he tore my town apart and put it back together again. It's a story about the men in our town who were killed in all the wars that this country has fought in, and the monument that Mick designed to help us remember them.

I knew Mick was different the first moment I laid eyes on him-- but I didn't think he was the artist Mrs. Langford had hired to build our monument. No, with his rear end hanging out of the window of the old dirty car, I was sure he was a pervert.

Come with me and find out who he really was—and who I turned out to be.

MAJOR IDEAS OR THEMES
Art is a way of looking at reality.

Life has a way of surprising us when we least expect it.

What's inside people is more important than what shows on the outside.

The first step in creating something is understanding whom you are creating it for.

Art can grow even from the seeds of war.

BOOK REPORT IDEAS
1. Describe the thoughts and feelings you had when you finished the book, explaining the impact that it had upon you and how and why your perspective has or has not changed as a result of reading it.
2. Discuss the idea that art is looking inside something or someone and revealing what is hidden there.
3. Discuss the idea that in order to make or build something for someone, you must first know them, know who they really are, on the inside.
4. "Art is what we find when the ruins are cleared away"—Katherine Porter. Explain how this quote pertains to the book. What were the ruins from which Mick's art came?

BOOKTALK IDEAS
1. Write your talk in the first person, speaking as Rocky.
2. Use a copy of the Degas painting Rocky talks about to illustrate your talk.
3. Write a character description talk as Rocky and Mick describe each other from the inside out.
4. Focus your talk on art and the definitions of it found in the book.

📖 📖 📖

MOTOWN AND DIDI. Walter Dean Myers. Dell, 1987, 174p., $3.95(pb); Viking, 1984, 174p. $12.95. HS. Eng, Soc Studies. Thoughtful; realistic fiction, romance.

SUBJECT AREAS
Blacks; Working; Friendship; Self-knowledge; Substance abuse; Rites of passage; Family relationships; Crime and delinquency; Homeless people; Peer pressure.

CHARACTERS
Motown: a 17-year-old boy who lives in an abandoned building in Harlem.

Didi Johnson: a teenager who wants to get a college scholarship so that she can escape from Harlem and her crazy, dependent mother.

Tony Johnson: Didi's brother, who is a drug addict.

Darlene Johnson: Didi's mother.

Tutmose Rogers: Motown's friend, a newspaper vendor.

Billy "Touchy" Jenkins: a drug dealer who is Tony's connection.

The Professor (Oliver Harris): a bookstore owner who gives Motown books and encourages him to better himself.

Carlos: Touchy's main boy.

Reggie and Lavelle: two of Touchy's boys. They try to beat Didi up after she goes to the police about Touchy.

Jimmy D.: another of Touchy's boys.

BOOKTALK
Seventeen-year-old Motown lives in an abandoned building, works at whatever jobs he can find, and dreams of getting out of Harlem. Didi studies as much as she can, takes care of her mother, who can't cope with the reality of her own life, worries about her drug-addicted brother, and dreams of getting out of Harlem. Both of them travel their roads alone, until one day they meet and their lives change.

But in Harlem there are no fairy tales, no happily-ever-afters, and it's dangerous to let someone into your life to share your dreams. Will Motown and Didi be able to let their love grow as strong as their hopes and dreams are?

MAJOR IDEAS OR THEMES
Hold fast to your dreams, because they are what keep you alive.

Sometimes you have to take the risk of trusting someone.

If you're willing to work and help yourself, you might find someone willing to give you a hand.

It is possible to overcome your environment, but it is not always easy.

Love can conquer evil, but not always.

Someone you love and who loves you can make life a lot easier.

You cannot determine the course of anyone else's life, no matter how much you may want to.

Ultimately, everyone is responsible for their own success or failure.

There is no honor among thieves.

BOOK REPORT IDEAS
1. Describe the characteristics of Motown and Didi that make them more likely to succeed in getting out of Harlem.
2. Speculate on where Motown and Didi will be in ten years and what their lives will be like.
3. Discuss what you think is the most important or memorable scene or event in the book and explain why you chose it.
4. There were a variety of relationships in this book that were at one time or another described as friendship. Describe each of them and show why or why not they were actually examples of friendship.

BOOKTALK IDEAS
1. Let Motown and Didi introduce themselves and their relationship, each of them speaking in the first person, one at a time.
2. Describe Motown and Didi briefly, and then focus your talk on the scene when they meet, when Didi almost gets beaten up. Be sure to explain why Touchy's boys are after her, leading up to a climax and leaving it unresolved.
3. The Professor knew Motown and Didi well and had a clear view of the situation with Touchy. In the first person, have him describe them, their problems, and their relationship.

📖 📖 📖

MY DANIEL. Pam Conrad. HarperCollins, 1989, 137p., $3.50(pb); HarperCollins, 1989, 144p., $12.95. JH. Eng, Am Hist. Quick read; historical fiction.

SUBJECT AREAS
Family relationships; Dinosaurs.

CHARACTERS

Ellie Summerwaite: the narrator, who was 12 at the time of the story.

Julia Creuth Summerwaite: Ellie's grandmother, who hunted for dinosaur fossils as a girl and now shares her experience with her grandchildren.

Daniel Creath: Julia's beloved older brother, who finds a dinosaur skeleton on their farm.

Stevie Summerwaite: Ellie's younger brother.

Charlie Summerwaite: Julia's youngest son and Ellie's father.

Jim Rhoades and Brett Holloway: two dinosaur hunters who camp on the Creath farm

Hump Hinton: a dinosaur hunter whom Jim and Brett warn Daniel about.

Amba: a woman who travels with Hump and seems to have psychic abilities.

BOOKTALK

"I loved my brother with a white fire. And like a burnt-out buffalo chip will crumble into dust if you stomp your foot beside it—that's what I was like once Daniel was gone."

It was a golden summer, the year I was 12 and Daniel was almost 16. I remember walking with him back from the fishing hole and thinking that it would always be like this, the two of us together. Nothing could ever hurt us or change that. How ironic it seems now, that at that same moment the dinosaur hunters were riding toward us, and their arrival was the beginning of the end.

They camped on our farm for nine days, and then they left, saying that there were no dinosaurs on our land. Daniel was sure he could find the dinosaur and kept searching. A paleontologist back East had offered a reward for a good find, and Daniel wanted that money to pay off our farm.

The next spring the rains came, heavy rains that washed away huge chunks of our creek bed, exposing what Daniel and I thought was the treasure of a lifetime. But the truth is, what came as a result of that find was worse than anything I could ever have imagined or dreamed of.

Is any treasure so special that it might be worth dying for?
(Based on a talk by Pam Swafford in *Booktalk! 4.*)

MAJOR IDEAS OR THEMES

People can share connections that last through many lifetimes.

As long as you remember someone, that person will never really die.

Great treasure is worth taking great risks to obtain.

Evil will eventually be punished.

A heritage that is passed from one generation to another need not be tangible to be important.

BOOK REPORT IDEAS
Look at the role of prescience, or foreshadowing, in the novel and show how it served to help increase tension and suspense.
1. Julia Creath did not see her brother's dinosaur until she was 80 years old. Discuss what you believe her reasons for waiting were and how or why she decided that it was time to see it.
2. Julia told her grandchildren things that no one else knew about, some of which were rather serious. Discuss her rationale for revealing them, for telling the whole story of Daniel's dinosaur.
3. Amba is a character who is mostly in the shadows. Show who she was, including how she ended up with Hump, and discuss her apparently psychic abilities. Decide if her actions toward Hump and the others in the novel were moral and ethical and defend your position.
4. Discuss the technique of flashback used in the novel and explain why you think it was or was not an effective way to tell Julia's story. (Hint: Try reading just the sections in the present, look at the story they tell, and then look at the ways they connect with the flashback sections.)
5. Discuss the last page of the book, when Julia once again sees Daniel. Explain what you think is happening here, including your rationale for your explanation.

BOOKTALK IDEAS
1. Using several dramatic quotes from the book, let Julia tell the story of that summer.
2. Tell the story from Ellie's point of view. Remember to only include information that she has at any one point rather than the full picture that Julia has.
3. Focus on Daniel, doing a character sketch of him and showing his passion for dinosaurs and his love for his little sister. This could be done in either the first or third person.

📖 📖 📖

NO DRAGONS TO SLAY. Jan Greenberg. Farrar, Straus & Giroux, 1984, 152p., $3.50(pb); Farrar, Straus & Giroux, 1984,

152p., $11.95. HS. Eng, PE, Sci, Archaeology. Average; realistic fiction, romance.

SUBJECT AREAS
Death and dying; Self-knowledge; Sports; Friendship; Science; Survival; Family relationships; Physical illness; Peer pressure.

CHARACTERS
Thomas Newman: a high school soccer star who discovers he has cancer.

Dr. Meyerson: Thomas's doctor, who diagnoses the cancer.

Sam and Sylvia Newman: Thomas's parents, who have a hard time dealing with his illness.

Ana Zacharian: an archaeologist who becomes Thomas's friend and confidant.

Nicky Zacharian: Ana's son, who also becomes Thomas's friend.

Penny Slater: Thomas's classmate, whom he meets again at an archaeological dig.

Milton Schwartz: an eccentric who does what none of Thomas's friends can do—he accepts Thomas's illness.

Pete Latham and Clark Rafferty: Two of Thomas's friends from the soccer team.

BOOKTALK
Thomas had been looking forward to soccer season all year. A junior, he was the star center for the varsity team. He didn't pay any attention when his body started to send him warning signs. He even managed to ignore the sharp, stabbing pain in his hip that kept him from playing as well as he usually did. But when he discovered a large, hard lump in his hip, he finally decided to tell his parents about it.

Dr. Meyerson didn't pull any punches. He told Thomas straight out that it was cancer, an inoperable and malignant tumor. The only treatment options were radiation and chemotherapy. The next 18 months would be hell, he warned, but if Thomas was lucky, at the end of the ordeal he would be cured.

The doctor hadn't exaggerated—the treatments were hell. The way his parents acted was hell. The way his friends suddenly disappeared was hell. The only person he could talk to was a friend of his mother's, an archaeologist named Ana. During a break in his treatments, she invited him to come out to the dig where she was working. That was great for a while. He made new friends and was learning a lot. But then the dig turned to hell, too. Thomas began to wonder if there was any way out for him. Was there any chance that he would ever be normal again?

MAJOR IDEAS OR THEMES

Being friends with someone means accepting all aspects of them, not just the ones you like or approve of.

Not every question has an answer.

When everything looks the blackest, it is most important to keep going.

Live in the present, not the past or the future.

Every ending is also a beginning.

Good things can come out of even the worst tragedies.

Friendship can only be given, not loaned.

You are the most important person you can know.

BOOK REPORT IDEAS

1. Show the ways that Thomas changed during the months covered by the book. Include both the way he saw himself and the ways he saw others.
2. Discuss what friendship means to you, basing some of your discussion on the insights Thomas gained about friendship from his relationships with Milton and Penny.
3. Discuss the meaning of the title. What dragons did Thomas want to slay? How did he succeed or fail?

BOOKTALK IDEAS

1. Focus your talk on the scene when Thomas learns he has cancer and how he reacts to the news.
2. Write a character description talk focusing on Thomas and his struggles in dealing with cancer and its effect on his life.
3. Speaking as Penny, describe Thomas, first as he was at the beginning of the book and then toward the end. Let her introduce him in such a way that your audience will want to meet him, too.

OF MICE AND MEN. John Steinbeck. Bantam, 1983, 128p., $2.95(pb); Random House, 1979, 208p., $11.95. HS. Eng, Am Hist. Thoughtful; historical fiction, classic fiction.

SUBJECT AREAS
Mental illness; Friendship; Working; Death and dying.

CHARACTERS
Lennie Small: a large, strong man with the mind and emotions of a
     child who works as a ranch hand or day laborer.

George Milton: Lennie's friend and traveling companion.

Candy: an old man who befriends George and Lennie and shares their
     dream of having their own farm.

Slim: the head ranch hand and an influential person on the ranch.

Carlson: one of the ranch hands.

The Boss: the owner of the ranch.

Curley: the boss's son, who is always spoiling for a fight.

Crooks: the black stable hand.

Curley's wife: a woman who flirts with most of the men on the ranch.

BOOKTALK
     When is killing someone a crime, and when is it a gift—or just
a mistake? Can someone who doesn't know the difference between
right and wrong be punished for committing a crime?
     Lennie was big and strong and gentle, with a child's mind and
emotions in a man's body. George, his friend and protector, kept him
out of trouble when he could and helped him escape from trouble
when he couldn't. He knew that Lennie didn't really mean to hurt
anyone or anything. The problem was, he just didn't know the extent
of his own strength or the difference between his strength and another's weakness. George knew how Lennie panicked if he didn't understand something or when people yelled at him—his first reaction
was to hold on tightly to whatever was in his hands.
     It was easy to protect Lennie when his frightened grasp killed
a mouse or a puppy. But what was George supposed to do when Lennie killed a human being? Could he be guilty of murder when he
didn't even know what murder was? Was George guilty, too, because
he refused to have Lennie put away knowing that locking him up
would be the same as killing him?
     These are questions you'll have to answer for yourself. What is
good? What is evil? What is the difference between right and wrong?
And finally, can someone who is innocent be capable of evil, or does
innocence carry its own morality?

MAJOR IDEAS OR THEMES
Everyone wants a home, a place to belong.

Sometimes you have to make a sacrifice for the sake of a friend.

Innocence has its own morality.

Is an act considered wrong by society always wrong, even if the person who does it has no idea what he or she has done?

Often the good and the innocent die because of the acts of people who are neither good nor innocent.

If someone you love has to die, maybe it is better to kill them yourself than to let somebody else do it.

BOOK REPORT IDEAS
1. A variety of situations in the book present moral dilemmas, such as the death of Candy's dog, the fight between Curley and Lennie, the death of the puppy, the death of Curley's wife, Lennie's death. Discuss the morality or immorality of one or more of these situations.
2. Lennie did many things without knowing their moral implications. Discuss whether an act that might be considered immoral for someone who recognizes it to be wrong would be immoral for Lennie or for someone else who does not know the difference between right and wrong.
3. Discuss the various deaths in the book and which of them were moral and which were immoral.
4. The story itself is very simple—discuss how that simplicity helps enhance its power.
5. Discuss the significance of the names Steinbeck used.
6. Discuss the role of the time period in the novel. In other words, could this same story have taken place at a different historical time?
7. Did George do the right thing in taking Lennie with him on the road? Would it have been more or less moral to have had him put in a home when his Aunt Clara died?

BOOKTALK IDEAS
1. Summarize the plot, leading up to an incident that you consider crucial. and end the talk before revealing its resolution.
2. Discuss the question of morality and which characters are and are not moral. Pose hypothetical questions for your audience.
3. Center your talk around a description of Lennie, including his strength and his innocent lack of awareness of it.

📖 📖 📖

ONE FAT SUMMER. Robert Lipsyte. Bantam, 1984, 150p.,
$2.50(pb); Harper & Row, 1977, 152p., $13.95. JH, HS. Eng.
Quick read; humor, realistic fiction.

SUBJECT AREAS
Working; Friendship; Self-image; Self-knowledge; Family relationships.

CHARACTERS
Bobby Marks: a 15-year-old boy who is very self-conscious about his
weight. He weighs over 200 pounds.

Joanie: Bobby's best friend. She is pretty except for her long, crooked
nose.

Pete Marino: a tall, tan lifeguard. He treats Bobby like a person instead
of a fat boy.

Mr. Marks: Bobby's father, who wants him to work as a day-camp
counselor.

Mrs. Marks: Bobby's mother.

Michelle Marks: Bobby's gorgeous older sister, who is dating Pete Marino.

Willy Rumson: a local ruffian who has a grudge against Bobby.

Dr. Kahn: the man who hires Bobby to take care of his lawn and pool
for the summer.

BOOKTALK
Bobby hated summertime. During the winter, he could hide
his fat under clothes, but in the summer he was exposed for all the
world to see. He'd stopped getting on the scale when it went past
200—he couldn't stand knowing how much he actually weighed. The
only time he felt like a normal person was when he was with Joanie.
He figured the reason they were best friends was that when they were
together, he felt thin and she forgot about her nose. The rest of her was
really pretty, but it seemed like no one else could see past her long,
crooked nose to find that out.

On the Fourth of July, though, Joanie told him she was going
back to New York for two weeks and wouldn't be able to work on their
summer project for school. She wouldn't tell him why. Bobby knew
he had to do something fast. His father was threatening to make him

be a junior camp counselor if he didn't find a job on his own. It was a relief when Dr. Kahn hired him to mow his lawn and take care of his car and swimming pool—until he actually started work. The first day was sheer torture. The second day was even worse. It turned out that Willie Rumson had had the job before him. Willie was an ex-Marine, mean, tough, and crazy, and determined to get even with Bobby, no matter what.

After that, whenever Bobby wasn't working, he was looking over his shoulder for Willie, and he didn't always look hard enough. One time Willie almost got him arrested, and another time he and his gang left Bobby on the island in the middle of the lake—stark naked! Could the Crisco Kid survive the summer, or would Willie and his pals melt him down before it was over?

MAJOR IDEAS OR THEMES
Changing your appearance can change the way people treat you.

Friendship does not depend on appearance.

Sometimes people have good reasons for the way they behave.

Changing your appearance—for better or worse—can change your self-image and your life.

Accomplishing a difficult task can make you feel better about yourself.

BOOK REPORT IDEAS
1. Explain why, when Joanie comes back with her new nose, Bobby feels bad about himself and starts to eat too much again. Describe what kinds of feelings he might have been having.
2. Bobby accomplished many things during that summer. Discuss what you think is the most important thing he accomplished and why you feel it was the most important.
3. Compare how Bobby felt about himself at the beginning of the summer and at the end, including the various events that helped him change his feelings.
4. Dr. Kahn treated Bobby unfairly. What things had to happen before Bobby was willing to stand up to him?
5. Speculate what will happen when Bobby and Joanie go back to school in the fall. How do you think other students will treat them? Why?

BOOKTALK IDEAS
1. Tell the story in the first person as if you were Bobby or Joanie.
2. Start your talk with one of the incidents Bobby has with Willie, showing what he had to put up with that summer. Then go back

and explain why it happened and what was going on with Bobby that summer.

3. Describe Bobby in detail and then describe his first day at work, leaving your audience in suspense about whether he will survive: "Will Bobby be able to make it through another day on the Lawn from Hell?"

📖 📖 📖

THE OTHER SIDE OF DARK Joan Lowry Nixon. Dell, 1987, 144p., $2.95(pb); Delacorte, 1986, 144p., $14.95. HS. Eng, Psych. Average; mystery, romance.

SUBJECT AREAS
Crime and delinquency; Peer pressure; Death and dying; Self-knowledge; Friendship; Family relationships; Physical illness.

CHARACTERS
Stacy McAdams: a teenager who awakens from a four-year coma and learns that she was shot by a burglar who also killed her mother.

Dr. Peterson: the doctor who treated Stacy while she was hospitalized.

Donna Kroskey: Stacy's older sister, who is now married and pregnant.

Mr. McAdams: Stacy's father.

Jan Briley: Stacy's best friend before the shooting.

Brandi Mayer: a reporter who sneaks into Stacy's hospital room for an interview.

Markowitz and Johns: detectives assigned to Stacy's case.

Jeff Clinton: a boy whom Stacy meets at a party. He seems strangely familiar to her.

Mrs. Cooper: Stacy's next door neighbor.

Tony Maconda: a friend of Stacy before the shooting.

Jarrod Tucker: a boy who used to live in Stacy's neighborhood.

Regina Latham: the district attorney who is handling Stacy's case.

BOOKTALK

When Stacy wakes up she feels like she's been having a long, long dream. She looks around and realizes that she's not in her own room but in a hospital room. She moves her hands and arms—everything seems to work all right, but then she raises her head and looks at her body. There is something terribly wrong. Her feet are much closer to the foot of the bed than they should be. "I'm only 13 years old," she thinks, "and I'm in the wrong body!"

What Stacy doesn't know and must now learn to accept is that four years ago she and her mother were shot by a burglar. Her mother died, and she has been in a coma ever since. She thinks that she's 13, but she's not—she's 17. Stacy is now faced with a new world full of strangers with familiar names. Her older sister, Donna, is now married and pregnant. Jan, her best friend, is beautiful, dates, knows how to wear makeup, and has a new best friend named BJ, who is really gorgeous! But Stacy doesn't want to learn to look like Jan and BJ, she just wants back the four years she's lost and the mother who's gone forever.

In her mind, she can see the man who shot her and she's sure she knows him, but she can't see his face or remember his name. She's the only witness, and when her story is in the newspapers and on TV, she realizes that now her killer also knows she will soon be able to identify him. Will she be able to remember in time, or will the killer find her first and end her life just as it's begun again?

(Adapted from a talk by Carol Kappelman in *Booktalk! 3*.)

MAJOR IDEAS OR THEMES

The human mind may try to protect itself by burying painful or traumatic memories.

After a tragedy or a great loss, all you can do is pick yourself up and go on.

Maturity means being able to cope with both the good and the bad parts of life.

A person who looks like an adult will be treated like one and expected to behave like one; similarly, someone who looks very young will be treated like a child.

You can't go back to the past; you can only go forward.

BOOK REPORT IDEAS

1. Discuss the conflict that Stacy felt when others treated her like a teenager when she felt like a little girl. Describe how she began to deal with that conflict and resolve it.

2. Describe some of the things that someone who has been asleep for four years might not know about, including both world events and little details such as the pasta salad that Stacy didn't want to eat because she didn't know what it was.
3. Discuss the responsibility of the media in a case like Stacy's when the publicity put her life in danger. Be sure to include the actions of the TV and newspaper reporters that are mentioned in the story. What does the First Amendment really mean in this kind of a situation?

BOOKTALK IDEAS
1. Focus your talk on when Stacy meets her family and friends again and realizes that she is the sole witness to her mother's murder.
2. Write your talk in the first person, speaking as Stacy.
3. Write part or all of your talk as if it were a newspaper story or a TV news broadcast.

📖 📖 📖

SEX EDUCATION: A NOVEL. Jenny Davis. Dell, 1989, 150p., $2.95(pb); Orchard, 1988, 150p., $13.95. JH, HS. Eng, Sci, Sex Ed. Thoughtful; realistic fiction, romance.

SUBJECT AREAS
School; Love; Friendship; Death and dying; Mental illness; Survival; Sex and sexuality; Family relationships.

CHARACTERS
Livvie Sinclair: a girl whose first love affair ends in tragedy.

David Kindler: Livvie's boyfriend.

Mrs. Fulton: a biology teacher who gives her class an unusual assignment.

Marie Kindler: David's mother, who is studying to be a minister.

Mr. Sinclair: Livvie's father, an IBM computer specialist.

Mrs. Sinclair: Livvie's mother, who works as an Avon representative.

Helen: a student in Mrs. Fulton's class and a longtime friend of David.

Maggie Parker: a lonely, pregnant woman who becomes the object of Livvie and David's "caring" assignment.

Dean Parker: Maggie's husband, a bitter and angry man who takes out his frustrations on her.

Hirsch: Livvie's psychiatrist.

BOOKTALK

Hirsch wants me to write down everything that happened, from beginning to end. He says it's the only way I can start to get well. The problem is, if getting well means remembering, I would rather be blind and crazy and stay here for the rest of my life. It just hurts too much. But Hirsch says I must, so I will.

My name is Livvie Sinclair. I'm 16 years old and the youngest person in this mental hospital. When they brought me here a year ago I couldn't see or speak, but one day I woke up and started to remember what had happened, and it hurt. It still hurts, but Hirsch says I have to remember anyway. But you remember, Hirsch—I don't want to get well!

It all started when I walked into Mrs. Fulton's ninth-grade biology class and saw David for the first time. I fell in love with him almost instantly, and I knew he loved me, too. Mrs. Fulton was teaching sex ed that semester, and David and I decided to work on our "caring" assignment together. We were supposed to find someone and care for them, do things for them. We were supposed to learn that sex is more than something physical, that it's also a joining, a sharing. And that's when everything began to go wrong. That's why I ended up here, why I decided to be blind and crazy. Sometimes caring hurts too much.
(Based on a talk by Joni Richards Bodart in *Booktalking the Award Winners: Young Adult Retrospective.*)

MAJOR IDEAS OR THEMES

Love cannot be demanded or earned. It must be freely given.

Great pain can change you completely, even take away your childhood. Such pain has to be put to use in some way, or it can destroy you, even though you go on living.

Blaming someone else for what has happened to you doesn't mean they are responsible. Nor does it help to accept blame for something that is not your fault.

Sometimes going insane is easier than dealing with a painful truth.

Most questions have more than one "right" answer. It all depends on your point of view.

Caring about someone means becoming vulnerable to them.

Sex is more than a physical act. It involves a mental and spiritual joining, and it is necessary to know yourself before sharing that self with someone else.

BOOK REPORT IDEAS
1. Discuss the things that David and Livvie could have done about Maggie and what the results of their acts might have been. Include your ideas about why they kept Maggie's life a secret.
2. Mrs. Fulton's teaching methods were unorthodox, but were they effective? Give examples of the things her students learned in class that they could not have gotten from a textbook.
3. Describe the person Livvie has become by the end of the book and show how that person differs from the one she was when she first met David.
4. Speculate on Livvie's life after the book is over. What will she take into adulthood as a result of her experiences? What kind of a person will she be and what kind of a life will she have?
5. Comment on Hirsch and his assignment requiring Livvie to remember and write down her story. Include why you think he did it and whether you think it had the effect that he intended.

BOOKTALK IDEAS
1. Use the prologue as a basis for your talk, showing Livvie's anger at Hirsch.
2. Using a character description technique, introduce both David and Livvie and show how they connected with each other.
3. Using a plot summary technique and starting with Mrs. Fulton's first class, sum up the plot, ending with a climactic moment. Be sure to bring a hint of Maggie's danger.
4. David and Livvie kept a secret far longer than they should have. Focus your talk on the idea of keeping versus not keeping secrets.

📖 📖 📖

SKINHEAD. Jay Bennett. Franklin Watts, 1991, 139p., $13.95. JH, HS. Govt, Eng, Psych. Quick read; realistic fiction, mystery, suspense, romance.

SUBJECT AREAS
Family relationships; Racism; Self-knowledge; Rites of passage; Friendship.

CHARACTERS
Jonathan Atwood: the rich, spoiled heir to the Atwood fortune.

Peter Atwood: Jonathan's grandfather.

Sgt. Tom Ward: a Seattle police officer who asks Jonathan to come to the bedside of a dying man.

Walter: the Atwoods' longtime family servant.

Jenny Mason: a beautiful, mysterious woman who asks Jonathan to stay in Seattle and help her fight the skinheads.

Carl: leader of the skinhead groups in the Northwest.

Mitch: a skinhead in Carl's group.

BOOKTALK
Late one night, Jonathan Atwood is awakened by a phone call on his private line, a number that few people know. The caller is a Seattle police officer who says that a dying man begged him to ask Jonathan to come to Seattle immediately. He refuses to explain who the man is or why he wants Jonathan to come, but it is obvious that he expects him to do so. Strangely frightened by the call, Jonathan obeys. He has no problem getting a first-class ticket on the next flight from New York to Seattle—one advantage of having a millionaire grandfather. But when he arrives, the man has died, taking his secret with him.

Jonathan decides to return home the next day, and his decision is reinforced by another phone call, this one threatening him with death if he stays in Seattle. At the airport, however, a beautiful woman named Jenny comes up to him and begs him to stay and help her. Attracted to her in spite of himself, he finally agrees. As they leave the airport, they are unaware that they are being watched by two skinheads.

"I don't like this," says one man. "He's dangerous to have around."

"But if he gets close?" asks the other.

"Blow him away."

"If he starts anything, he's dead meat."

"Like Kaplan?"

"Like him."

Jonathan soon realizes that he is in the middle of a mystery. But what he doesn't know is that the next death might be his own.

MAJOR IDEAS OR THEMES
Racism is wrong.

Sometimes people in your own family turn out to be strangers.

Be true to yourself and your beliefs, even when doing so is difficult or painful.

Your family members are not necessarily the people who are closest to you and understand you the best.

BOOK REPORT IDEAS
1. Explain what you think Jonathan will do with his inheritance when his grandfather dies, including your rationale for your opinion.
2. Identify the man on the plane whom Jonathan talks to and explain his importance.
3. Discuss the differences between Carl and Mitch. Examine the reasons for these differences and how the book would have been different if they had been the same kind of person.
4. Compare how you think Jonathan felt about his family and his life when he left his grandfather's house to the way he felt before the phone call from Sgt. Ward.
5. Explain the importance of Walter in Jonathan's life and the role he played in it.

BOOKTALK IDEAS
1. Tell the story from Jonathan's point of view, focusing on the fears and urges that he had.
2. Tell the story from Mitch's point of view—be careful not to include things he could not have known.
3. Use the different elements in the story to interest someone in reading it—the phone calls, the Skinheads, Sgt. Ward, Jenny, Peter Atwood, Walter, and Jonathan's growing suspicions.
4. Focus on the things Jonathan felt, overheard, or dreamed about as a way to build suspense in the listener.

📖 📖 📖

SLAKE'S LIMBO. Felice Holman. Macmillan, 1986, 128p., $3.95(pb); Macmillan, 1974, 126p., $12.95. JH. Eng, Psych. Quick read; realistic fiction.

SUBJECT AREAS
Runaways; Working; Self-knowledge; Survival.

CHARACTERS
Aremis Slake: a small boy who lives in terror of gangs. When things get too rough on the street, he often escapes to the subway.

Willy Joe Whinny: a subway motorman whose route goes by Slake's hiding place.

The Pink Cleaning Lady: one of Slake's newspaper customers, who gives him an old jacket and a pair of jeans.

The Man with the Turban: another newspaper customer, who asks Slake where he gets the papers that he sells.

The Manager: the man who runs the small coffee shop in the subway station. He gives Slake a job sweeping up.

The Waitress: a woman who works in a restaurant that Slake sometimes visits. She occasionally gives him food.

BOOKTALK
Aremis Slake is the kind of person everyone picks on. He's small and wears glasses, and he can't join a gang because he gets sick every time he tries to smoke. In the tough section of New York where Slake lives, not being in a gang means getting beaten up regularly. Too small to fight back, Slake counts on speed to escape. When he's attacked, he runs into the nearest subway station to hide. Usually he ends up riding on trains until he thinks things have cooled down in the neighborhood and he can go home.

One day it seems as though everyone in the city is after him—the bullies who take his sweater, the cop who catches him climbing a tree in the park, and the subway attendant who sees him duck under the turnstile. Desperate, he can think of only one place to run—down the tracks and into a subway tunnel. Knowing he can't stay on the tracks, he finds a hole in the tunnel wall, sort of a cave, and moves in. Safe in his hiding place, he realizes that he doesn't want to go back upstairs to the real world, and so he doesn't—for 121 days.

This is the story of how Slake survived in the underground world of New York's subway system, and what finally happened to bring him up to the surface again.
(Adapted from a talk by Richard Russo in *Booktalk! 2.*)

MAJOR IDEAS OR THEMES
There is a place in the world for everyone.

You can't hide from life forever. Sooner or later you have to go back and face it.

Survival is possible even under difficult circumstances, if you are creative and make the most of your opportunities.

Providing people with a necessary service makes you valuable to them and can make money for you as well.

BOOK REPORT IDEAS
1. Explain the meaning of the bird in Slake's chest. What is it a metaphor for?
2. Examine Slake's relationships with the people he makes friends with in the subway and show how they are unique and similar.
3. At the end of the book, Slake has something to do before he goes back into the subway. Discuss what you think he intends to do, basing your answer on his other actions throughout the book.
4. Discuss the various symbols in the book and their meaning, for example, the rose-colored glasses, the bird, and the rat.
5. Compare Slake at the beginning and the end of his stay in the subway, showing how he changed, what he learned, and why.
6. Discuss the importance of Willy Joe Whinny and explain why the author included the sections about him, his feelings, and his dreams.

BOOKTALK IDEAS
1. Focus your talk on the idea of survival and interest your audience by telling them one or two of the things Slake has to do to survive, both before and after he went into the subway for 121 days.
2. Let Slake tell his own story, using his thoughts rather than his spoken words, because he actually says very little in the book. Get into his head and look out through his eyes.
3. Describe Slake in detail, explaining his appearance and why he ran to the subway so often. End with a sentence that lets your audience know he finally went into the subway and didn't come up for 121 days.

📖 📖 📖

SNOW BOUND. Harry Mazer. Dell, 1975, 144p., $3.25(pb). JH, HS. Eng, Soc Studies. Average; realistic fiction.

SUBJECT AREAS
Survival; Friendship; Family relationships; Runaways.

CHARACTERS
Tony LaPorte: a spoiled, self-centered 15-year-old who spends much of his time daydreaming.

Cindy Reichert: an aloof and lonely girl who has trouble making friends and talking to people. She sometimes thinks that she is too smart for her own good.

Fred LaPorte: Tony's father, who wants his children to have a better life than he has had.

Bev LaPorte: Tony's mother, who shares her husband's dream of a better life for their children.

Evie, Donna, and Florence: Tony's equally spoiled older sisters.

Arthur: a large, brown mutt that Tony wants to adopt.

BOOKTALK

Tony was furious! His parents had no right to kick Arthur out just because the dog had made some noise. If they'd agreed to let him keep it in the first place, he wouldn't have had to sneak him into the basement, and all this would never have happened. Tony began plotting his revenge. He would steal his mother's car and go to his Uncle Leonard's. No one would know where he was, and his parents would be panic-stricken—just like he wanted.

A little way outside of town Tony picked up a hitchhiker, figuring he could use some company. It was an act he quickly regretted. Cindy was stuck-up and thought she knew everything, and if he'd known what was good for him he would have passed her right by. Then he wouldn't be in this mess.

Miss know-it-all Cindy hadn't believed he knew where he was going, and the next thing he knew she had grabbed the steering wheel and he'd lost control of the car. Now the car was wrecked and his parents were going to kill him. This was not what he'd had in mind at all! Now they had no choice but to sit and wait for someone to come along and rescue them.

Only nobody came, and it began to dawn on Tony and Cindy that they had gone farther off the road than they realized. And by then the blizzard had started, and pretty soon it was obvious that help wasn't going to come for days, if at all. It was up to the two of them to figure out how to survive, and how to save themselves. If they don't, all their rescuers will find is the old Plymouth, with two frozen bodies inside.

MAJOR IDEAS OR THEMES

A crisis can bring out the best or the worst in a person.

Determination and creativity can help a person survive against great odds.

Sometimes people must cooperate in order to survive, regardless of how they feel about one another.

In a life or death situation, everything but survival becomes secondary.

When you are forced to depend only on yourself for survival and succeed, you gain tremendous strength and self-confidence.

It is easier to see yourself clearly in a life and death situation, although you may not like what you see.

BOOK REPORT IDEAS
1. Show how Tony and Cindy changed as a result of their ordeal.
2. Discuss the meaning of Cindy's statement, "We gave birth to ourselves."
3. When life is stripped down to the essentials, the meaning of morality and ethics changes. Explain how this is shown in the hook.
4. Compare the things that were most important to Cindy and Tony at the beginning and the end of the book.
5. Speculate on what might have happened after the end of the book. Do Cindy and Tony stay friends? How do you think their lives will be different because of their experience? How will their being changed by what happened to them affect their family? (Remember, when one member of a group or system changes, the whole system has to change to accommodate that difference.)

BOOKTALK IDEAS
1. Use either Tony's or Cindy's voice to tell the story, speaking in the first person.
2. Focus your talk on the question of survival and on what one must do to survive.
3. Center your talk around the scene leading up to the crash, ending it with their realization that they are lost and the car is ruined.
4. Using quotes from both Tony and Cindy, show their personalities and some of the conflicts between them. End by posing the question, "Can these two people ever learn to cooperate so they can survive together, or will they each go their own way and die apart?"

📖 📖 📖

SOMETHING UPSTAIRS: A TALE OF GHOSTS. Avi. Avon, 1990, 128p., $2.95(pb); Orchard/Watts, 1988, 128p., $11.95. JH. Eng, Am Hist. Quick read; supernatural, mystery.

SUBJECT AREAS
Ghosts; Time travel.

CHARACTERS

Kenny Huldorf: a small, thin boy who meets a ghost in the attic of an old house.

Avi: the narrator of the story, who believes Kenny's tale is true.

Mr. and Mrs. Huldorf: Kenny's parents, who move from L.A. to Providence, Rhode Island, where they buy an old house.

Caleb: the ghost who shares Kenny's attic room and demands that Kenny help him find his murderer.

Pardon Willinghast: a historian who can move between the present and the past. He holds the key to the mystery of Caleb's death.

BOOKTALK

Kenny and his parents had just moved to Providence and bought an old historic house. The attic had been fixed up for Kenny. There were two rooms off the attic, and the smaller of them had a large dark stain in the middle of the floor. When Kenny saw it, he somehow knew it was blood, and that someone had been killed in that room. He put a box of books on top of the stain to cover it up, and made sure that the door to the room was always shut. A few nights later, Kenny was waked up about two o'clock in the morning by a noise from the small room. When he opened the door, he saw two ghostly hands rising from the stain and pushing the box of books off it. When the stain was uncovered, the hands pushed the rest of the ghost's body out of the stain, and he stood up and began to search the room, when he saw Kenny standing in the doorway.

His name was Caleb, and he was a slave who had been killed in that room in 1800. He wanted Kenny to come into the past with him and find out who killed him and how he could prevent his own death. It wasn't until Kenny agreed to go with him that he discovered he wasn't the only one who could travel in time—a man he knew as a historian in the present was really a slaver from the past, and he knew how to keep Kenny in the past forever.

Avi says, "This is the strangest story I've ever heard. I think it's true." But it isn't Avi's story, it's Kenny Huldorf's, just as Kenny told it to Avi. Kenny's story, Avi's words. Decide for yourself if it's true or not.

MAJOR IDEAS OR THEMES

Bitter memories can live on after death.

Friendship can conquer evil.

Taking a risk and trusting someone else can benefit both of you.

Every problem has more than one solution.

If something in the past changes, the present changes as well.

BOOK REPORT IDEAS
1. Find out if there is really a Stillwell House in Providence and how much else about this story might be true.
2. Discuss the ways that Kenny and Caleb are products of their own times.
3. Discuss the character of Pardon Willinghast and how he was able to control Caleb and his past and therefore control Kenny as well.
4. Explain why you think Avi told the story in the way that he did, as if it were true, and whether you believe that it is. Be sure to defend your stance, using quotations from the book to help you do so.
5. Discuss the relationship between Caleb and Kenny and how their friendship changed both of them.

BOOKTALK IDEAS
1. Speaking as if you were Kenny, talk about your meeting with Avi and the story you told him. Make sure it sounds as if it were really true.
2. Tell Caleb's story from his point of view, starting with the first time he saw Kenny.
3. Center your talk around the first few times Kenny saw Caleb and how he decided to help him.

📖 📖 📖

STRANGE ATTRACTORS. William Sleator. Dutton, 1990, 169p., $13.95. JH, HS. Eng, Sci. Quick read; science fiction, adventure.

SUBJECT AREAS
Time travel; Friendship; Self-knowledge; Ethics.

CHARACTERS
Max: a teenaged boy who visits a science lab and obtains a device that lets him travel through time.

Sylvan: the scientist who invented the phaser that allows people to travel through time. Actually there are two Sylvans, and Max must figure out which is the good one and which the evil.

Eve: Sylvan's daughter, who also exists in two versions.

BOOKTALK

What would you do if you had the power to go anywhere you wanted, in any time you wanted, just by pushing a button? When Max tried it, he found it exciting, more exciting than anything he had ever experienced. He couldn't resist trying it again—and again.

But Max soon discovered that not everyone who travels in time is honest, or ethical. Some of the people he met looked like people he already knew. They even had the same names. But they came from different timelines, and they had different goals and agendas. What's more, Max began to suspect that one of their agendas was—Max himself.

Was the experience of time travel so powerful, so irresistible, that Max would risk anything—his own life, even the lives of everyone in his timeline—to do it just one more time?

Travel in time with Max and discover just how much of a strange attractor that trip can be.

MAJOR IDEAS OR THEMES

Power corrupts, and absolute power corrupts absolutely.

Chaos, once begun, can quickly get out of control and take over.

You alone are responsible for your actions.

What people do, and how they defend or justify their actions, tells you more about them than what they say.

Excitement and danger are more interesting and intriguing than predictability and consistency.

The present can be complicated and difficult enough to handle without worrying about the past or the future.

BOOK REPORT IDEAS

1. Discuss the idea of time travel as it is presented in the book, including the idea that moving in time will create chaos that will eventually become uncontrollable.
2. Explain the process Max went through to decide which Eve and Sylvan were the real ones and which were the false ones.
3. Based on information from the book and your own interpretation of it, explain what you understand a strange attractor to be.
4. Show how Max changed during the course of the book and detail the reasons for these changes.
5. Compare and contrast the explanation of time travel and its dangers as explained in this book and in the three *Back to the Future* movies.

6. Speculate on what you think will happen when Max finishes his own phaser and goes forward in time to meet the false Eve.

BOOKTALK IDEAS
1. Using a plot summary technique, tell the story up to the point when Max realizes that there are two Eves and two Sylvans.
2. Focus your talk on the journeys in time, both to the past and to the future.
3. Have both the true and the false Eves introduce Max and show the differences between them in their views of him.

A SUMMER TO DIE. Lois Lowry. Bantam, 1979, 120p., $2.95(pb); Houghton Mifflin, 1977, 154p., $13.95. JH, HS. Eng, Psych, Art. Quick read; realistic fiction.

SUBJECT AREAS
Death and dying; Family relationships; Self-knowledge; Photography; Friendship; Aging.

CHARACTERS
Meg Chalmers: a teenager who is interested in photography and dreams of being famous someday.

Molly Chalmers: Meg's pretty, popular, and self-assured older sister. She wants to make a career of being a wife and mother.

Dr. and Mrs. Chalmers: Meg and Molly's parents.

Will Banks: the owner of the small country house that the Chalmers rent so Dr. Chalmers can finish his book.

Ben Brady and Maria Abbott: Will's other tenants. They are unconventional free spirits who ask Meg to photograph the home birth of their baby.

Happy William Abbott-Brady: Ben and Maria's baby.

Tierney McGoldrick: Meg's steady boyfriend.

BOOKTALK
I remember when Molly drew the line down the center of our room and said, "Now be as much of a slob as you like, but keep your

mess on your side of the room." It was unlike Molly to be so angry, but I paid attention to the dividing line and kept my things on my side of it. It made it even more clear how very different we were—Molly was the pretty, popular one who wanted to grow up to be a wife and mother. I was the smart one with glasses and a camera, who wanted to grow up to be someone other people would look up to.

But that winter we were different in another way too—Molly was sick all the time and spent a lot of time at home curled up on the sofa, with a box of Kleenex nearby in case her nose started to bleed again. I was the one who was out doing things, meeting new people, making friends.

Molly was better in the spring, but soon it was obvious that we were different in yet another way—Molly was never going to get well. I was the one who was going to live—she was the one who would die before any of her dreams came true. It's hard to let a sister go. I know—I had to do it.

MAJOR IDEAS OR THEMES

Often other people can see good in us that we aren't able to see ourselves.

Just because you fight with someone doesn't mean you don't love them.

Friendship has nothing to do with how old either person is.

Being true to yourself means first learning and then accepting who you are.

Value the ways in which you are different from other people in your family.

Dying is not the worst thing that can happen to you—but doing it without grace or dignity may be.

In the end, everyone must die alone.

As long as you remember someone and think of them with love, they do not die.

You have to go on after a tragedy. You cannot cry forever.

BOOK REPORT IDEAS

1. Discuss the relationship between Meg and Molly and how Molly's sickness changes it.
2. Discuss how it might feel to know that you will die before your plans and dreams of what you will do as an adult can come true. How do you think you would be similar to or different from Molly?

3. Look at the different kinds of friendship that are portrayed in the book and how various characters were helped by their friends.
4. Meg learned many lessons in this book. Explain what you think some of those lessons were, quoting what she says about them. (To help you get started, some of these lessons are given in the "Major Ideas or Themes" section.)
5. People show love for each other in a variety of ways. Look at some of the ways characters in this book love each other and how they express this love. Remember, love is not limited to romantic love, but also includes love for friends and family.
6. Discuss the symbolism of the quilt in the story. Include why you think Lydia started it, the significance of the pieces she included in it, and why you think it was finished when it was.
7. There are several quotes from Dr. Chalmers's book in the story. Why do you think they were included, and what do they mean in the story and to you?

BOOKTALK IDEAS
1. Write your booktalk in the first person, from either Molly's or Meg's point of view.
2. Create a dialogue between Molly and Meg so that they tell the story between them. Use some of the conversations they had, their thoughts, or what you think they might have said.

THE WILD CHILDREN. Felice Holman. Penguin, 1985, 149p., $4.95(pb); Macmillan, 1983, 160p. $12.95. JH. Eng, W Hist. Thoughtful; historical fiction.

SUBJECT AREAS
Friendship; War; Survival; Other countries; Homeless people.

CHARACTERS
Alex: a 12-year-old Russian boy who wakes up one morning to find that his family has been taken away by the secret police.

Katriana Sokolova: Alex's teacher, who helps him get to Moscow to find his Uncle Dimitri.

Peter: the leader of the gang of wild children that Alex joins when he gets to Moscow.

Boris, Kostia, Ivan, Leon, Miska, Grigory, Basil: the other boys in the gang.

Anya: a girl who wants to join the all-boy gang.

Basil Sergyevitch Sokolov: Katriana's brother, who helps people escape from Russia.

Nicholai: a sailor who lives on the coast of Russia and helps many people get out of the country.

BOOKTALK

They were everywhere in Russia—the wild children, the homeless ones whose parents were dead or gone or too poor to support them. They lived in cellars, on the streets, anywhere they could. To survive, they stole, begged, even sold places in the bread lines.

Never in his wildest dreams did Alex think he would become one of the wild children. But then he woke up one morning to find that the life he had known had vanished overnight. His whole family had been taken away by the secret police. Somehow the soldiers had missed Alex's room, which was little more than a cubbyhole. He had escaped capture, but now how would he survive?

The only person Alex trusted was his teacher, Katriana, who gave him the money for a ticket to Moscow, where he hoped to find his uncle. But the first night his satchel was stolen, and when he finally reached Moscow his uncle was nowhere to be found. He was alone, penniless, freezing, and starving. When he met Peter, one of the wild children, he didn't have much choice—it was either join the gang or die in the streets. Alex didn't know then that joining Peter's group was his first step toward a life he could not even imagine, on a road that he didn't know existed.

Where did the road lead, and what waited at the end of it?

MAJOR IDEAS OR THEMES

When life gets down to essentials, people will do whatever they need to do to survive.

Life on the streets has its own set of ethics and its own moral code.

Helping others when you can may ensure that they will be willing to help you in the future.

Loyalty and trust can exist even among thieves.

Sometimes survival is largely a matter of choice. You find what you need because you are looking for it.

Freedom is worth any price.

BOOK REPORT IDEAS

1. Compare the wild children of Russia and the street kids of today, looking at how they are similar and how they are different.
2. Compare the moral code of someone on the edge of survival and someone who has either all or most of what they need. How and why did the ethics code in Peter's gang differ from the codes of other gangs?
3. Describe the characteristics of Peter's gang that made it a family.

BOOKTALK IDEAS

1. Write your talk in the first person from Alex's point of view.
2. Focus your talk around the idea of homeless children who live on the streets, comparing Alex's world with what is happening today.
3. Summarize the plot, leading up to the first time Alex goes to the cellar with Peter.

WOLF OF SHADOWS. Whitley Strieber. Fawcett, 1986, 128p., $3.95(pb); Delacorte, 1986, 128p., $14.95. JH, HS. Eng, Hist, Govt. Quick read; science fiction, adventure.

SUBJECT AREAS

Animals; End-of-the-world scenarios; Friendship; War; Survival.

CHARACTERS

Wolf of Shadows: a large, black wolf who grew up at the edge of the pack and who is now trying to lead it to safety after a nuclear war.

The Gray Wolf: an old wolf who is the pack's former leader.

The Gray's Mate: a proud and beautiful wolf who eventually becomes the Wolf of Shadow's mate.

The Human Female: an animal ethologist who escapes from the city with her two daughters just after the first bomb is dropped.

The Young Female: Sharon; she and her mother become members of the pack led by the Wolf of Shadows.

The Burned Female: Carol, Sharon's sister, who dies soon after they meet the wolf pack from burns she received when the city was bombed.

BOOKTALK
In the 1950s, the world lived under the constant threat of nuclear war. Many people built bomb shelters in their back yards, and school children were taught to crawl under their desks for protection if "the Bomb" was dropped. Today the threat of nuclear war is smaller than it has been in decades. If such a war did happen, though, what would it be like for the residents of the planet who have nothing to do with human quarrels? What would the animals do and how would they survive?

Because of his great size, the Wolf of Shadows had never been accepted by the rest of the pack. He had lived nearer human places than the others, and although he didn't understand what had happened, he knew that the silver streaks in the sky and the huge mushroom-shaped cloud on the horizon meant danger to the wolves. When there were no more animals to hunt, he gathered the pack and took them south, where he sensed they might find safety. Two new members of the pack followed closely behind and shared in the wolves' kills—a human female and her young daughter. Would the pack survive the nuclear winter? Would they be able to escape the desperate and dangerous human survivors who threatened them? What might animals do in the aftermath of nuclear war? Follow the Wolf of Shadows and find out.

MAJOR IDEAS OR THEMES
The leader protects the weaker members of the pack.

War is harmful to all living things.

Times of stress and adversity may seem to bring out the bad sides of people more often than the good.

Creatures of different species can become friends if they respect one another.

All living things have a drive to survive.

BOOK REPORT IDEAS
1. Discuss the process that made the two humans members of the pack. Include both what the wolves and what the humans did during this process.
2. Compare this book to other books about nuclear war and its aftermath and show how the effects are the same and different for humans and for animals.
3. With the exception of the woman and her daughters, the only humans the wolves met in the book could be considered to be bad or evil—at the least, having more negative than positive characteris-

tics. Discuss the idea that adversity more frequently brings out the bad than the good in people.

BOOKTALK IDEAS
1. Write the talk in the first person as if you were the Wolf of Shadows.
2. Illustrate your talk with a picture of a wolf who looks like the Wolf of Shadows.
3. Focus your talk on the relationship between the humans and the wolves and perhaps write it in the first person, speaking first as the Wolf of Shadows and then as the woman as they describe each other and their trek.
4. Use some of the author's comments in the afterword as part of your talk.

WORDS BY HEART. Ouida Sebestyen. Bantam, 1983, 144p., $2.95(pb). JH, HS. Eng, Am Hist, Sociology. Thoughtful; historical fiction.

SUBJECT AREAS
Blacks; Racism; School; Family relationships; Friendship; Love; Death and dying; Working; Rites of passage; Crime and delinquency; Secrets.

CHARACTERS
Lena Sills: a determined girl who can win a Bible-quoting contest but can't make her classmates see beyond her dark skin.

Ben Sills: Lena's father, a strong and gentle man who believes in turning the other cheek and letting God reward the righteous and punish wrongdoers.

Claudie Sills: Lena's stepmother and the mother of Roy Armilla and the baby.

Mrs. Chism: the Sills's landlady.

Mr. Haney: a white sharecropper for Mrs. Chism. He hates the Sills because they are Black and because Ben is honest and a better worker than he is.

Tater Haney: the oldest Haney child, who wants to prove that he is a big man.

Sammy Haney: Tater's little brother, who is teased by the boys at school.

Winslow Starnes: Lena's main opponent in the Bible contest. He learns to see past Lena's dark skin to the person inside.

Jaybird Kelsey: the man who sets up the Bible contest and furnishes the prize for the winner.

Mr. and Mrs. Doans: the schoolteachers.

BOOKTALK
Lena can use her "Magic Mind" to win a Bible-quoting contest and make her beloved father proud of her, but can she win against the prejudice that says a black family doesn't belong in Bethel Springs? Can she prove that she is as good as anyone else, regardless of the color of her skin? Can her gentle father stand up against the rifle-toting Haneys, who hate him and his family for exposing them as bigots?

Ben fights back with love and won't let Lena fight back with anything else. But will love be enough to turn aside the hatred of the Haneys and the scorn and dislike of the whole town?

MAJOR IDEAS OR THEMES
People are all the same inside, regardless of the color of their skin.

Respect is the first step toward seeing someone else as your equal.

Forgiveness requires more strength and courage than revenge.

When you love someone, you want them to be proud of you.

Strength can be born of tragedy when one decides not only to survive, but to triumph.

When you steal, you rob not only the person you stole from, but the people who trusted you.

Loving your enemies and being kind to people who hurt you is far easier said than done.

BOOK REPORT IDEAS
1. Compare the feelings and actions of the whites in this book with the way minorities are treated today. Show how much has changed and how much hasn't.
2. Whether someone wins or loses is not always as obvious as it might seem. There are several instances of winning and losing in this book: the Bible-quoting contest, Ben's confrontation with Mrs. Chism, the manner of his death, Winslow's actions both at school

and at the Sills's, and Claudie's reaction to Ben's death. Show how the winners in these incidents lost and how the losers won.

3. Discuss what Lena proves to herself and to the world when she refuses to reveal who killed Ben.

4. Describe the kind of person you think Lena will grow up to be and what kind of philosophy or ethics she will teach her children.

5. Define freedom and describe how it is seen and enacted in this book.

BOOKTALK IDEAS

1. Focus your talk on the first scene in the book, the Bible-quoting contest, and how it ended.

2. Using a character description technique, focus your talk on Lena and on her anger.

3. Contrast some of the Bible verses Lena quoted with her feelings and actions later on in the book.

📖 THIN 📖

THE ACCIDENT. Todd Strasser. Delacorte, 1988, 192p., $14.95. JH, HS. Eng, PE. Thoughtful; realistic fiction, romance.

SUBJECT AREAS
Death and dying; Substance abuse; Sports; Ethics; Self-knowledge.

CHARACTERS
Matt Thompson: a teenager who decides to investigate the cause of a car accident that killed his best friends.

Karen Shecter: Matt's girlfriend, who understands his need to know what really happened in the accident.

Bobby Stewart: a wealthy daredevil who loves to party and always includes his friends.

Jason Ellman: the only survivor of the wreck. He doesn't want Matt to know the truth.

Randy Chapman and Susie Zorn: the girls who date Jason and Bobby and who are with them the night of the accident.

Chris Walsh: Matt's next door neighbor, a rebel who drinks heavily and deals drugs.

Mrs. Thompson: Matt's mother.

Peter Thompson: Matt's 12-year-old brother.

BOOKTALK
Matt stares at the newspaper article, unable to accept what it says. Three of his best friends are dead, killed by a drunk driver—one of the school burnouts. He knows that he could have been in that car—he had been with them at the party the night before, and if he hadn't had to go throw up he would have gone with them.

"Why?" he asks himself over and over. "Why them and not me?" He wants to know what really happened that night. But Jason, the only survivor, won't talk to him, and the police seem determined to accept the obvious answer—they were all drunk, but Chris was driving, so the accident was his fault. Except, Matt thinks, the pieces don't fit together. Something is missing, and he's determined to find out what it is, even if no one else will help him.

What Matt doesn't realize is that once he knows the truth, he will have to decide what to do with it. Is it moral to tell the truth when doing so will hurt people who have already been hurt enough and will ruin many others? Is it ever ethical to tell a lie or to keep silent about what you know in order to benefit people who would otherwise suffer?

How do you define right and wrong, moral and immoral? It's hard enough when your decision affects only your own life, but Matt's decision will affect thousands.

MAJOR IDEAS OR THEMES

Being true to yourself is the most important thing in life.

Sometimes a lie can be as beneficial, or as moral, as the truth.

Each of us must decide whether to tell the truth as we see it or keep quiet and avoid hurting someone who doesn't deserve to be hurt.

Going along with the crowd can sometimes be deadly.

Envy hurts the person who envies, not the object of the envy.

BOOK REPORT IDEAS

1. Discuss the various moral dilemmas found in the book and your reaction to them. Do you agree with the ways they are resolved or not, and why?
2. Discuss the relationship between Bobby and Matt and Jason and Matt, showing how they were different and how they were similar and looking at the causes for these differences.
3. Compare what happened after the wreck with what might have happened had Matt been the survivor, not Jason. Include a discussion of why Jason decided to tell the story he told, based on his personality and his relationship with Bobby.
4. In the end, Matt made a decision. Discuss whether you might or might not have made the same decision and why.

BOOKTALK IDEAS

1. Without giving away the ending, use the ideas of right, wrong, moral, immoral, and ethics in your talk, posing questions that make your audience think about their own ethics.
2. Discuss the idea of change in the book and how a small decision can change the rest of your life—such as Matt's decision to go to the bathroom just when he did, which kept him out of the wreck that night, or his decision to continue looking for the truth when everyone tried to make him stop.
3. Write your talk in the first person, letting either Matt or Karen tell the story.

📖 📖 📖

ACE HITS THE BIG TIME. Barbara Murphy. Dell, 1982, 192p., $3.25(pb). JH, HS. Eng, Art. Quick read; realistic fiction, humor, romance.

SUBJECT AREAS
Gangs; Friendship; Family relationships; School; Working; Movies; Self-knowledge; Peer pressure.

CHARACTERS
Horace (Ace) Hobart: a 16-year-old who is about to enter JFK High School in Manhattan with a new name, a new look, and a new gang.

Nora Hobart: Ace's little sister, who warns him about the Purple Falcons.

Raven Galvez: the most beautiful girl Ace has ever seen. She introduces him to the Purple Falcons.

Freddy Cruz: the leader of the Purple Falcons.

J. D. Jackson, George Wyciewski, Tony (Slick) Vaccaro: the members of the Purple Falcons.

Webber: a hotel clerk who is willing to take messages for Ace.

Flo and Barney Hobart: Ace's long-suffering parents.

Calvin Feckleworth: Horace's best friend from New Jersey.

Uncle Jake: Barney Hobart's brother, who isn't always on the right side of the law.

Piranhas, Wart-Hogs, Monsoons: rival gangs in New York City.

BOOKTALK
Horace stared at the ghastly sight in his bathroom mirror. It was his first day at JFK High School, in Manhattan, and he had a sty the size of an egg yolk. His little sister had already warned him about the Purple Falcons—"They're gonna cream you, Horace." But when he came out of the bathroom, she took one look and said, "They're not gonna cream you, Horace, they're gonna kill you! "

Things only got worse after that. His mother couldn't find a brown paper sack, so she packed his lunch in a clear plastic bag. He couldn't find his jean jacket and had to wear the one his uncle had sent him from Japan—red silk, with a dragon on the back! "At least the pockets are big enough to put my lunch in," Horace thought, so the bagel went in one pocket and the banana in the other. But what was he going to do about that sty? Then he saw Nora's Halloween makeup box—maybe there was something there—a black eye patch—perfect! Now if he could just keep out of the way of the Purple Falcons, he'd have it made.

As luck would have it, however, he ran into the Falcons as soon as he got to school. After that, he was certain he would never survive the day. But Horace discovered that appearances can be deceiving, and a bagel, a banana, a dragon, a brand-new Bic ballpoint pen, and a black eyepatch all combined to give Horace a new look, a new name, and a new career. After all, the Purple Falcons had never seen Horace before, and they came to some very different conclusions about why he looked the way he did that morning.
(Adapted from a talk by Joni Richards Bodart in *Booktalk! 2*.)

MAJOR IDEAS OR THEMES
You can't always depend on first impressions.

Appearances can be deceiving.

You can be tough and still make the honor roll.

When you start at a new school, you have an opportunity to be anyone you want to be. You don't have to be the same person you were at your old school.

It's easier to look tough than to be tough.

BOOK REPORT IDEAS
1. Compare the impression that Ace made on the Purple Falcons the first day at school and the impression that he thought he would make or was making.
2. Discuss what you think the purpose of the Purple Falcons was; why they existed.
3. Compare the Falcons to the students in your school. Are there any who are like the Falcons? If not, why not?
4. Discuss the idea of first impressions and their importance in making friends and starting at a new school. Show how sometimes first impressions are made stronger and how sometimes they are overcome or changed.
5. Discuss the idea of "becoming someone else" when you start at a new school or with a new group and include the variety of things that you would have to consider when doing that. Show how effective this might or might not be.

BOOKTALK IDEAS
1. Write your talk in the first person from the point of view of Raven or one of the other Falcons, giving their impressions of Ace on his first day of school.
2. Write part of your talk as if it were an excerpt of a newspaper story about the gangs at JFK High.
3. Write your talk in two parts, one from Horace's point of view and one from the Falcons' point of view as they meet each other on the first day of school.

CANYONS. Gary Paulsen. Doubleday, 1990, 184p., $14.95. JH, HS. Eng, Am Hist. Average; realistic fiction, historical fiction.

SUBJECT AREAS
Native Americans; Self-knowledge; Crime and delinquency; Rites of passage; Family relationships; Working; Death and dying; Philosophy.

CHARACTERS
Brennan Cole: a 15-year-old runner who enjoys solitude.

Coyote Runs: an Apache boy who was murdered by white soldiers during the 1860s.

Mr. Homesley: a teacher who believes what Brennan tells him about the skull and is willing to help him.

Mrs. Cole: Brennan's mother, a lonely woman who loves her son but doesn't understand him.

Bill: Mrs. Cole's current boyfriend, who leads the trip to the canyon where Brennan finds the skull.

Stoney: the old man for whom Brennan works.

BOOKTALK
Brennan was a loner, a runner, and a realist. He didn't believe in ghosts or spirits until after he found the skull. Then he began to hear a strange voice in his mind, asking him to do something—something urgent, something important. But what?
Coyote Runs was almost a man when he joined his first raid against the bluebellies, the soldiers who were trying to take away the Apaches' homeland. The raid was a great success, and the warriors

were nearly home when he and his best friend, Magpie, met a group of soldiers. Magpie was killed, and Coyote Runs was wounded. He knew he would never be able to reach the sacred place of his ancestors, where his spirit would be able to rest with his people. Then a bluebelly soldier put a gun against Coyote Runs's forehead and pulled the trigger.

More than a century later, Brennan was haunted by his find. He knew that somehow he and the skull's original owner were connected and that he was responsible for carrying out that person's last wishes. But how was he to discover whose skull it was and what he was supposed to do with it? And once he knew, how was he to accomplish the task, especially because he knew that it was a felony to take anything from a national park? Would the spirit of Coyote Runs be able to rest at last, or would his skull end up in a museum display case?

MAJOR IDEAS OR THEMES
Crossing the boundary from childhood to adulthood always means facing difficult challenges and making hard decisions.

Many events and things in the world cannot be explained by science or logic.

Each of us has a store of inner strength that we can draw on in times of difficulty or hardship.

Our lives can change in a single instant, even though we might not realize the change has taken place.

Some adults, and some parents, understand and trust teenagers. They are therefore willing to help them, even when the help needed is unusual or unique.

Some obligations are more important than obeying the law.

BOOK REPORT IDEAS
1. Discuss the difference in the way that Brennan's mother understood him and the way that Mr. Homesley did. Show how both these people loved Brennan and wanted to help him although they did it in very different ways.
2. Think about what kind of a person Brennan was and why who he was allowed him to acknowledge the message of the skull. Describe Brennan as if he were a friend of yours, elaborating on what the book says about him. The mental description is of more importance here than the physical one.
3. Show how Brennan and Coyote Runs were similar even though they lived hundreds of years apart. Be sure to look at both mental and physical similarities.

4. Discuss what you think Brennan learned from this experience and how you think his life will be different in the future because of it. Speculate on what he might be like in five or ten or more years and what he might be doing.

BOOKTALK IDEAS
1. Use a picture of a skull or a young Apache brave as a prop for your talk.
2. Write the talk the way the book is written, from both Brennan's and Coyote Runs's points of view. This talk could be done in either the first or third person.
3. Let Brennan tell his story, using only the portions of the book from his point of view, up to one of the climactic moments, such as when he learns that the skull is that of an Apache boy about his own age, or when he learns whose skull it really is.

ⅧⅧⅧ

THE CONTENDER. Robert Lipsyte. HarperCollins, 1987, 176p., $2.50(pb); Harper & Row, 1967, 190p., $12.89. HS. Eng, PE, Soc Studies. Thoughtful; realistic fiction.

SUBJECT AREAS
Sports; Blacks; Substance abuse; Working; Self-knowledge; Friendship; Peer pressure; Crime and delinquency.

CHARACTERS
Alfred Brooks: an orphaned high school dropout who hopes that boxing will give him a way to get out of Harlem.

James: Alfred's best friend, a drug addict who is caught robbing the store where Alfred works.

Hollis: a friend of James who was in on the robbery.

Major: another friend of James.

Henry Johnson: a man who helps out at the boxing gym in Alfred's neighborhood.

Aunt Pearl: the relative who has cared for Alfred since his parents' death.

BOOKTALK

"James, are you crazy man? You can't shoot that stuff and live man! What do you think, you the only one with problems? You think I like working in that grocery store my whole life?"

Alfred Brooks knew that he would never become an addict like his best friend, James, but he didn't know where his future lay. He only knew that it lay outside Harlem, where he lived with his aunt and his three cousins, and outside the grocery store where he spent all his time after he dropped out of high school.

He climbed the stairs to the third-floor gym uncertainly. Maybe this was a crazy idea. Maybe he'd train like a dog and then get his brains knocked out in his first fight. Maybe, but he had to try. He had to get out. He had to.

"I'm Alfred Brooks. . . . I come . . . to be . . . a fighter."

(Adapted from a talk by Dee Scrogin in *Booktalk! 3*.)

MAJOR IDEAS OR THEMES

Drugs don't solve problems, they create them.

Some rewards are not worth the pain it takes to achieve them.

Before you can be a champion, you have to be a contender.

True courage means going ahead even when you are afraid.

It is more important to prove your worth to yourself than to prove it to anyone else.

Just because you disapprove of something someone has done doesn't mean you can't still be friends.

BOOK REPORT IDEAS

1. Discuss the changes that Alfred makes in himself during the course of the book.
2. Explain what you think is the most important thing Alfred learned from boxing and why you chose it.
3. Speculate on how you think Alfred will turn out in the future—what kind of a man he will be in ten or fifteen years. Be sure to give your rationale or justification for the changes you think will occur in him and in his life.

BOOKTALK IDEAS

1. Focus your talk on the scene when Alfred goes to look for James, leading up to James's arrest and Alfred's decision to try boxing as a way out.
2. Write your talk as if you were Donatelli and describe Alfred both as a person and as a boxer.

❑❑ ❑❑ ❑❑

DON'T LOOK BEHIND YOU. Lois Duncan. Dell, 1989, 179p., $3.50(pb); Delacorte, 1989, 179p., $14.95. HS. Eng, Govt, Psych. Quick read; realistic fiction, romance, mystery.

SUBJECT AREAS
Family relationships; Crime and delinquency; Self-knowledge; Peer pressure.

CHARACTERS
April Corrigan: a high school junior and star tennis player.

Bram Corrigan: April's brother, who is in the third grade. He has one blue and one brown eye.

Steve Chandler: April's boyfriend.

Mrs. Corrigan: April's mother, a well-known author of children's books.

Mr. Corrigan: April's father, an airline employee who is also an undercover informant for the FBI.

Mr. Loftin: an airline executive who is on trial for drug smuggling.

Sherry Blaugrand: April's best friend.

Lorelei Gilbert: April's grandmother.

Max Barber: April's father's best friend since childhood.

Jim Peterson: one of the Corrigans's bodyguards. He dies saving their lives.

Mike Vamp: a hitman who works for Loftin.

Rita Green: the woman who makes the relocation arrangements for the Corrigans.

Larry Bushnell: the captain of the Grove City tennis team.

Kim Stanfield: Larry's cousin.

Tom Geist: the Corrigans's Florida contact with the U.S. marshals.

BOOKTALK
April's life ended one Tuesday afternoon in May. That morning she'd awakened in her own room and lay in bed looking at the formal she planned to wear to the prom in just a few days. She'd got-

ten up and brushed the long blond hair that was one of her trademarks, and when she left for school she carried the tennis racket that was another trademark—she was one of the team's stars. But she never went to the prom or to graduation parties with her boyfriend Steve, and it was a long time before she played tennis again. She never saw her bedroom after that day—the day her life came crashing down.

It happened because her father was testifying against a major drug dealer, and the FBI discovered that a hit man had been hired to find and kill April, her parents, and her little brother. To save their lives, the Corrigans had to go into the Witness Protection Program. That meant they had to give up their old identities and take on new ones. Each of them had to give up or get rid of the things that made them unique and recognizable. April's long hair was chopped off with a pair of nail scissors. Her little brother had to wear contacts so no one would notice that his eyes were different colors, and her mother had to give up a successful career as a children's author.

Forget about the past, they were told. Don't even think about it. But April couldn't forget. She missed Steve and all her friends. Surely, she thought, it couldn't hurt just to send him one little letter. But how was she to know the letter would be intercepted by the gunman who was out to kill them, or that her small mistake would put the family that used to be named Corrigan in mortal danger?

MAJOR IDEAS OR THEMES
Who you are inside is not based on how you look or what you do.

It is possible to rebuild your life from nothing, but it's not easy.

You can't go home again. If you do, you'll find that life has gone on for the people you left behind, and that they are not the people they were when you left.

A small mistake can have enormous consequences.

Thinking of yourself first can have dangerous or tragic consequences for those who are close to you.

Each person is unique. No one else quite like you has ever lived or ever will.

BOOK REPORT IDEAS
1. Discuss what it might be like to go into the Witness Protection Program and have to leave everything that is familiar to you behind, disappearing without a trace. Be sure to include what could be the benefits of doing this, as well as the difficulties.
2. Compare April when the book began with the person she was when it ended. Describe what you think she learned from her experiences.

3. Discuss the idea of individuality and how each of us is unique and different. Explain how giving up these things would affect someone's self-image.
4. Speculate what April and her family will be like in the future. Will they ever be able to go back to being the people they were before, and if they are not, how will this affect them?

BOOKTALK IDEAS
1. Focus your talk around the idea of giving up everything that makes you who you are—appearance, activities, friends—and becoming someone else.
2. Write your talk in the first person, speaking as April as she describes the upheaval she and her family must go through.
3. Focus your talk on the scene when April finds out that she has to leave her home and friends without any good-byes.

📖 📖 📖

THE EXECUTIONER. Jay Bennett. Avon, 1990, 176p., $2.95(pb). JH, HS. Eng, Psych. Thoughtful; mystery, suspense.

SUBJECT AREAS
Friendship; Death and dying; Family relationships.

CHARACTERS
Bruce Kendall: a teenage boy who is severely injured in a car accident that kills his best friend. He is the only one who knows that he caused the crash.

Ray Warner: Bruce's best friend, who was driving the car that crashed.

Oliver Warner: Ray's older brother.

Dan Warner: the sheriff, who is Ray and Oliver's father.

Ed Millman and Elaine Ross: friends of Ray and Bruce who encouraged Bruce to keep drinking with them at Carlson's bar. They were not injured in the crash.

Carlson: the owner of the bar where the teens were drinking.

The Executioner: the one who kills.

BOOKTALK

"I am the executioner. When the crime is committed and the Lord God does not take vengeance nor does the exalted State move to declare and then to punish, I say when these bitter events happen, then comes the time for the executioner to declare himself or herself as the case may be. I have waited long enough.

"So the time has come and I declare myself the executioner.

"The three criminals are hereby sentenced to death. By fire. By water. By earth."

Slowly a hand descended, picked up the white sheet of paper that was in the box, and held it to the shadowed light. Slowly two words were read aloud.

"By fire."

The executioner smiled. "The first shall die by fire."

It had finally begun, and only the executioner knew where it would end.

MAJOR IDEAS OR THEMES

Revenge solves little and frequently hurts the person who achieves it more than the person it was directed against.

Once you have made a mistake, you cannot undo it, no matter how badly you want to. "The moving finger writes and having writ moves on, nor all your piety nor wit shall lure it back to cancel half a line, nor all your tears wash out a word of it." (The Rubaiyat of Omar Khayyám, st. 71.)

People will not listen to what they do not want to hear.

In the final analysis, forgiving yourself is more important than anyone else forgiving you.

BOOK REPORT IDEAS

1. Discuss the identity of the executioner, including your speculations on when and why he was created, the purpose of the bank vault, and what would have happened to him had he not been caught.
2. Look at the effect of guilt on Bruce and how it changed the way he saw himself and his life. In your opinion, was Bruce the only guilty one, or were others partially or equally to blame for Raymond's death, including Raymond himself?
3. No matter how much Bruce wished he could have died in Raymond's place or prevented Raymond from dying, he cannot change the past. Compare his situation to similar situations in other books you've read, and discuss how you would handle such a situation.
4. Discuss the meaning of friendship as it is seen in the book, including which of the characters were true friends and how the

story would have been changed if everyone who said "I'm your friend" had really acted like it.

BOOKTALK IDEAS
1. Use the notes written by the executioner to introduce your talk or to help add suspense to it.
2. Talk about the book as much as possible from the executioner's point of view. Because you know who he is, remember to be careful not to give away his identity.
3. Use the quote from Omar Khayyám to introduce the idea that you can't always go back and fix your mistakes, and from that lead into the story.
4. Use Bruce's thoughts as the main body of your talk, letting him tell the story based on his memories and his fears.

THE FACE ON THE MILK CARTON. Caroline Cooney. Bantam, 1990, 184p., $14.95. JH. Eng, Soc Studies. Average; realistic fiction, romance.

SUBJECT AREAS
Runaways; Kidnapping; Self-knowledge; Family relationships; Friendship; School.

CHARACTERS
Janie Johnson: a 15-year-old who recognizes a "missing child" photo on a milk carton as herself.

Sarah-Charlotte Sherwood and Adair O'Dell: Janie's two best friends.

Reeve Shields: Janie's next-door neighbor and boyfriend.

Megan, Lizzie, and Todd Shields: Reeve's intelligent and overachieving brother and sisters,

Frank and Miranda Johnson: the couple Janie has always known as her parents.

Mr. and Mrs. Shields: Reeve's parents.

BOOKTALK
How would you feel if you were having lunch with your friends in the school cafeteria and suddenly saw a picture of yourself

on the back of a milk carton? Yourself as a 3-year-old, and under-neath a caption saying you were stolen from a shopping center in New Jersey twelve years ago. Everyone at the table thinks you're jok-ing, but you're not—you remember that dress, and later you realize that you can remember the shopping center and walking away with someone who was going to buy you an ice cream sundae.

That's what happened to Janie. She's 15, a sophomore in high school, with parents who love her and a totally normal life—until she sees that picture. She doesn't know what to do—does this mean the parents she loves so much stole her from somebody else? Will she have to go live with people she doesn't love, doesn't even remember? Even Reeve, the only person she dares talk to about it, says she should just forget it and concentrate on being Janie Johnson. But she can't. The memories get stronger and stronger. She wants to know who she really is, but how can she send the only family she has ever known to jail for kidnapping?

She knows she has to do something, but what?
(Original talk by Joni Richards Bodart appeared in *Booktalk! 4*.)

MAJOR IDEAS OR THEMES
Your true parents are the ones who raised you.

It is better to know the truth than to be ignorant, even when the truth hurts.

Some problems have no good solutions, and the only way to deal with them is to choose the solution that will do the least damage.

Your best friend is the person you can trust with your deepest secrets.

In the end, you are who you define yourself to be.

Real life may not have any happily-ever-afters.

BOOK REPORT IDEAS
1. Reeve's and Janie's families are very different. Show how their families have affected the way these two teenagers feel about themselves and their lives.
2. Janie is torn between staying with the parents who raised her and finding the family from which she was kidnapped. Discuss what she fears she will have to give up and what she would gain if she went to live with her original family.
3. Explain why you think the author chose to end this book at the point at which she did.
4. Speculate about what happened to Janie, her parents, and Reeve after the last page of the book.

5. Discuss the kind of parents the Johnsons were and how their parenting affected the decisions that Janie had to make. Include both their good points and their weaknesses as parents.

BOOKTALK IDEAS
1. Take a milk carton with a little girl's picture on it with you to use as a prop.
2. Use Janie's flashes of returning memory as the basis of your talk, connecting them with just enough other information to make sense.
3. Write your talk in the first person from Reeve's point of view, letting him tell about Janie and her problem.

📖 📖 📖

A FAMILY APART. Joan Lowry Nixon. Bantam, 1988, 176p., $2.95(pb). JH. Eng, Am Hist, Govt. Quick read; historical fiction, adventure.

SUBJECT AREAS
Adoption; Runaways; Crime and delinquency; Family relationships; Stepparents; Friendship; Self-knowledge.

CHARACTERS
Frances Mary Kelly: a 13-year-old who is the oldest of the Kelly children. She works with her mother to help support the family.

Megan Kelly: the 12-year-old, who watches the younger children while Frances and their mother are at work.

Mike Kelly: the 11-year-old, who commits the theft that gets the whole family in trouble.

Danny Kelly: the 10-year-old, who wants to be just like Mike.

Peg Kelly: the red-haired, freckled 7-year-old, who wants only to stay with her sisters and brothers.

Petey Kelly: the 6-year-old baby of the family.

Charles Loring Brace: the founder of the orphan train.

Andrew MacNair: the scout who travels ahead of the orphan train, looking for families to adopt the children.

Jake and Margaret Cummings: the people who adopt Frankie and Petey.

Mr. and Mrs. Alfrid Swenson: the couple who adopt Peg and Danny.

Emma and Benjamin Browser: a brother and sister who adopt Megan.

Mr. and Mrs. Friedrich: the couple who adopt Mike.

BOOKTALK

Frances couldn't believe it—her little brother Mike was a thief! But she'd seen it with her own eyes, watched him pick a man's pocket and run into an alley. She followed him. "You stole that man's money. You're a thief! What if you get caught, what will you do then?"

"I won't," Mike sneered, "I'm too clever." But just as he spoke, a shadow fell across them, and a policeman grabbed Mike by the shoulder.

"Is he the one?" he asked the man standing behind him.

"Yes, that's the little thief!" Mike was arrested, and Frances just barely got away.

When she told her mother what had happened, she said she'd take care of it, but she wouldn't tell Frances how. It wasn't until the next morning when they all went to court that she found out how her mother had kept Mike out of prison. She had agreed to give all six of her children to the man who ran the Orphan Train. She would never see her children again.

It was 1860, and in New York City, hundreds of orphans and homeless children roamed the streets, with no place to go and no one to take care of them. Out West, there were families who needed and wanted to have children to help them settle the land. Charles Loring Brace decided to gather up these unwanted children in New York, and send them by train to the states in the West where there were families who could adopt them and give them a better life than the one they had on the streets of New York. These trains were called Orphan Trains, and Frances, Mike and their four brothers and sisters were put on the next one out of New York.

The last thing that their mother said to Frances was, "Take care of Petey—don't let him forget me." But girls were hard to place—the family that wanted Petey might not want her. Then Frances suddenly thought of a way to make sure that she was there to keep her promise to Ma. She cut off her hair, and dressed in her brother's clothes, and became Frankie, not Frances, because a family that wouldn't take a girl and a boy might be willing to take two boys!

What will happen to the Kellys? What if they are adopted by families at different stops—will they ever be together again?

MAJOR IDEAS OR THEMES
A single wrong act can have unexpected and far-reaching consequences.

The time when it is hardest to believe in yourself is the time that you need to believe the most.

All people are created equal, regardless of the color of their skin.

Belief in a positive future will help you survive present troubles.

Courage is doing what is right in spite of your fear.

You can do almost anything if you set your mind to it, whether other people believe in you or not.

Sometimes deception is necessary to benefit a good cause or to help someone else.

Sometimes breaking an unfair law is the right thing to do.

Sometimes you must sacrifice your own happiness to help someone you love.

BOOK REPORT IDEAS
1. Compare the homeless children of the 1860s and the 1990s, showing their similarities and their differences. Is there an "orphan train" for children today? Why or why not? (Hint: Don't limit your discussion to the United States.)
2. Discuss the idea of loving sacrifice as it is portrayed by several of the characters in the book.
3. Compare the lives that Frankie and Petey had on the frontier with the ones they, and the other Kelly children, might have had if they had stayed in New York.
4. Many of the real orphan train children are now trying to find the families they were separated from. Locate one or more of these stories and compare it to this book. Does this book seem to portray reality?

BOOKTALK IDEAS
1. Illustrate your talk with old pictures of children from the 1860s, or a poster used to advertise the arrival of the orphan train.
2. Write a character description talk, introducing each of the six children and describing them and their situation briefly.
3. Focus your talk on the idea of homeless children and compare the Kellys to children one might find on the streets of many countries today.
4. Focus your talk on two scenes: when Mike steals the wallet and is caught, and in the courtroom when the children find out what their mother has decided to do.

📖 📖 📖

FELL. M. E. Kerr. Harper & Row, 1988, 176p., $3.25(pb); Harper & Row, 1987, 160p., $12.95. HS. Eng, Psych. Quick read; realistic fiction, romance.

SUBJECT AREAS
School; Self-knowledge; Friendship; Secrets; Crime and delinquency; Family relationships; Rites of passage.

CHARACTERS
John Fell: an average high school junior who is offered $20,000, and perhaps $30,000, to pretend he is someone else.

Woodrow Pingree: a wealthy man who wants John to impersonate his son.

Fern Pingree: an artist, she is also Mr. Pingree's wife and boss.

Woodrow Thompson Pingree: Woodrow Pingree's son, who is nicknamed Ping.

Helen Keating (Keats): John's girlfriend.

Mrs. Fell: John's mother, who loves to shop.

Jazzy Fell: John's five-year-old sister.

BOOKTALK
It was like getting a $20,000—maybe a $30,000—scholarship. All Fell had to do was impersonate a nerd for two years. He didn't even hesitate before he said yes. It was a way out, the ticket to a future that up until now had seemed an impossible dream.

What Fell didn't know was he would also unexpectedly become a member of the Sevens, an exclusive club whose members enjoyed almost unlimited power and prestige both on campus and after graduation. He also didn't know the real motive behind that offer of $20,000, or what might actually happen if he took the money.

If you're thinking you'd be willing to switch identities for $20,000, maybe you ought to read Fell's story before you accept the check.

MAJOR IDEAS OR THEMES
Mere chance can be a powerful force, bringing us either great reward or great sorrow.

People are frequently not who they seem to be.

Infatuation is usually based only on a person's appearance.

You are responsible for the choices you make in life.

Details count, whether you are impersonating someone else or investigating a murder case.

There is no point in being honorable with a dishonorable person.

Telling the truth can sometimes get you into trouble.

BOOK REPORT IDEAS
1. Discuss the ethics of what Fell did and why he was willing to do it. Explain why you would or wouldn't be willing to do the same thing.
2. Discuss the idea that our lives are ruled to one extent or another by mere chance. Give examples from the book and from your own experiences.
3. How did Fell see himself? Describe Fell as he would have described himself.
4. Describe the Sevens, and explain why the club existed and what its overt and covert purposes at Gardner were.

BOOKTALK IDEAS
1. Illustrate your talk with a $30,000 check or a group of seven things.
2. Center your talk around the idea of sevens, and use several lists of sevens in your talk—such as the seven details that changed Fell's life or one of the sevens that new members had to recite.
3. Focus your talk on the idea of secrets or of pretending to be someone else for money.

THE GIRL IN THE BOX. Ouida Sebestyen. Bantam, 1989, 182p., $3.50(pb); Little, Brown, 1988, 166p., $12.95. JH, HS. Eng, Psych, Writing. Thoughtful; realistic fiction, mystery.

SUBJECT AREAS
Survival; Self-knowledge; Kidnapping; Friendship; Family relationships; Writing.

CHARACTERS
Jackie McGee: a girl who is kidnapped and locked in a concrete room.

Brian and Carol McGee: Jackie's parents.

April Beckner: Jackie's best friend.

Zack: a friend of Jackie and April.

Miss Flannery: Jackie's English teacher.

No-Face: the man who kidnaps Jackie.

BOOKTALK

"TO ANYONE WHO FINDS THIS: My name is Jackie McGee. I am kidnapped. Please notify Brian and Carol McGee and the police immediately. This is not a joke."

It all happened so fast. One minute I was fighting with April, shouting at her and chasing her down the street. The next minute a man in a ski mask jumped out of a parked van and shoved me inside. He brought me here, to this dark, square place with concrete walls. The only light comes from a crack near the door. He shoved me down some stairs, so I think it's probably a cellar.

I've lost track of how long I've been here. My kidnapper hasn't come back. I found some food and some water, so it looks like he planned on keeping me here awhile. I also have a typewriter and some paper that he threw in after me. So while I wait for someone to find me, I write. I write letters to myself, to my parents, to April, to Zack, telling them how I feel and how much I love them. I write notes that I poke through the crack by the door, not knowing where they will land or whether anyone will find them.

I just hope that someone finds me soon. Before I run out of food. Before I run out of water. Before I run out of time.

MAJOR IDEAS OR THEMES

Words said in anger are often repented in leisure.

Too much dependence can ruin a friendship.

Life is not always fair, nor does it always provide the answers we would like to have.

You can survive even in the worst situations if you keep calm and stay in control of yourself.

Even best friends don't know everything about each other.

It's important to be honest with your friends, even when it hurts.

BOOK REPORT IDEAS

1. Discuss the style the author used in this book. It is written in many connected fragments. Are some of these more real or more gripping than others? Why or why not?

2. Jackie used a story form to explain what happened between herself, April, and Zack. Explain why you think she used this device and how her perspective of what occurred changed because of it.
3. Discuss your ideas about why the author left the ending unfinished. What do you think she was trying to say, and how did you react to her message?
4. Speculate on what you think happened after the end of the book, and discuss why you believe either that Jackie lived or that she died.
5. Jackie learned many lessons during her time in the box. Discuss which you think was the most important one, explaining why you think it was so important for her.

BOOKTALK IDEAS
1. Write the talk as if you were Jackie.
2. Use bits and pieces of Jackie's writing to explain what is happening and why.
3. Write the talk as if you were a newspaper or TV reporter investigating Jackie's disappearance.

📖 📖 📖

HATCHET. Gary Paulsen. Penguin, 1988, 195p., $3.95(pb). JH. Eng, Soc Studies, Psych. Thoughtful; realistic fiction, adventure.

SUBJECT AREAS
Survival; Family relationships; Divorce; Self-knowledge; Animals.

CHARACTERS
Brian Robeson: a teenager who is stranded in the wilderness after a plane crash.

Mr. and Mrs. Robeson: Brian's parents, who have recently divorced.

The Pilot: the man who was flying Brian over the Canadian wilderness.

BOOKTALK
When Brian climbed into the cockpit of the bush plane, he wasn't thinking about the flight. He was thinking about his parents, wondering whether he should tell his father what he knew about his mother's secret—the secret that was the reason they had gotten the divorce. So he wasn't paying any attention to the pilot as they took off and began their flight over the Canadian wilderness.

Just about the time Brian realized something was wrong with the pilot, the man screamed and jerked and clutched at his chest.

Suddenly, Brian was alone in the tiny two-seater plane with a dead man. He couldn't reach anyone on the radio, and he knew that the plane would run out of gas soon. When that happened, he would crash, and he'd have no control over where the plane went down. It seemed to him that it would be better to crash the plane himself, so that he could at least choose the spot.

He landed in a lake and escaped before the plane settled too deeply into the water. But he was hurt, and everything that he had had with him in the plane was gone. All he had were the clothes on his back and the hatchet his mother had given him just before he left. He wouldn't have had that if she hadn't made him put it on his belt before he got out of the car. It had seemed like a silly present at the time, but now the hatchet was the only thing he had to help him survive. Would it be enough?

MAJOR IDEAS OR THEMES
When life gets down to the bare essentials, priorities change.

Sometimes in order to survive you have to draw on everything you have learned in your life.

The biggest obstacles you have to overcome are your own fear and inertia.

Survival depends both on luck and on your ability to make use of that luck.

It is possible to learn valuable lessons from one's mistakes.

Fighting for survival changes you both mentally and physically.

BOOK REPORT IDEAS
1. Discuss the changes that Brian went through in the woods, first physical changes and then mental changes.
2. Brian went into the woods with only the hatchet and learned to make a number of tools to help him survive. Discuss how he figured out which tools he needed and how he learned to make them.
3. Brian knew when he came out of the woods that he was a new and different person. Describe the new Brian and compare him to the old one.
4. Brian thought a great deal about his parents and the secret while he was in the woods. What did he finally decide about them?
5. Luck played a part in Brian's survival. List some of the times Brian was lucky and made luck work to his advantage.

BOOKTALK IDEAS
1. Write your booktalk about the first part of the book, leading up to the death of the pilot and leaving Brian alone in the plane with a dead man.
2. Focus your talk on one of the dangerous encounters with animals that Brian had while he was in the woods.
3. Write your talk by interspersing newspaper headlines about Brian with what he is actually doing in the woods.

HERE AT THE SCENIC-VU MOTEL. Thelma Hatch Wyss. Harper & Row, 1989, 192p., $3.25(pb); Harper & Row, 1988, 192p., $11.95. JH, HS. Eng. Thoughtful; realistic fiction, humor, romance.

SUBJECT AREAS
Family relationships; School; Working; Self-knowledge; Friendship; Peer pressure.

CHARACTERS
Jake Callahan: a high school senior who is placed in charge of the other six teenagers from Bear Flats who are rooming at the Scenic-Vu Motel.

Jordy Callahan: Jake's little brother and a born poet.

Martin Rawley: a 16-year-old who thinks he is a psychologist and never takes off his hat.

Drift Davis: a smart aleck with a big mouth and lots of freckles.

Mona Robbins: a 16-year-old with short black hair.

Netty Robbins: Mona's 14-year-old sister.

Helen Burgoyne: a 14-year-old who always carries a bedraggled stuffed animal.

Mrs. Christensen: Jake's English teacher.

George and Angel Callahan: Jake and Jordy's parents.

Mrs. Matz: the owner of the motel, otherwise known as Mrs. Scenic-Vu.

BOOKTALK

This wasn't how Jake had imagined his senior year, riding herd on six younger kids from Bear Flats, just because the school board was too cheap to send a bus to pick them up every day. Monday through Friday, they lived at the Scenic-Vu Motel—which had no view at all, much less a scenic one. Friday afternoon the bus took them all back to Bear Flats for the weekend.

Being on their own in a motel sounded good in theory. In practice it was something else. Because Jake was the oldest, he was in charge. He made only two rules: study hard and have fun. He figured he wouldn't have time to enforce any more than that, and he was right!

All in all, it was quite a year. First there were the girls from town who arrived at midnight with a case of beer, ready to party. Then there was the Pop-Tart bake sale at school to pay for the damage done when they almost burned the motel down. Finally, there was the beautiful baby blue 1970 Thunderbird that Jake found in the motel garage. And don't forget the smaller details, like the grungy stuffed animal Helen insisted on sleeping with, Martin's smelly socks that seemed to turn up everywhere, and Jordy's sleepwalking on the highway in the middle of the night. Take all that, and you have the makings of a senior year that Jake could never have imagined in his wildest dreams.

All he wanted was a pickup truck and a girlfriend from town. Wait till you see what he got instead!

MAJOR IDEAS OR THEMES

People who love you for yourself are better company than people who love you for what they think you have.

With hard work, anyone can succeed.

Some things in life are more important than being popular.

Some people get so involved in looking for someone to love that they overlook the one standing right next to them.

Honesty and genuineness are far more important qualities than good looks and popularity.

The person who enforces the rules is the one who gets to decide what they mean.

Success has more to do with motivation than with innate intelligence.

BOOK REPORT IDEAS

1. Jake interpreted his two rules in a variety of ways in order to keep the Bear Flatters in line. Discuss the other rules that he enforced based on his interpretation of his first two.

2. Jake set two goals for himself that year—motel management and popularity in school. Discuss the ways in which he reached and failed to reach his goals and how he felt about them at the end of the school year.
3. The Bear Flatters changed a lot during the year they spent in the motel. As Jake said, "They went from dumb to smart real fast." Describe how each of them changed and what lessons they learned that caused those changes.
4. Describe the role Mrs. Matz played in the book, including both what role she was expected to play and how and why that role expanded during the year.

BOOKTALK IDEAS
1. This book is written as a journal for Jake's senior English project. Use excerpts from the journal to form your talk, making sure your audience knows that you are quoting from his journal. You can do this in the first few quotes you use, when he is talking to his teacher, or you can do it in a brief introduction to your talk, when you explain what Jake did and what you will be doing.
2. Focus your talk on Jake's two rules and the various permutations of them. For instance, how did Jake use the rules to make the Bear Flatters study, keep them from eating junk food, persuade them to pay him gas money, and so on? In-troduce the situation and then use the rules to help you tell the story.
3. Let each of the Bear Flatters and Mrs. Matz introduce themselves and their own view of the situation. Jake should probably be the last one to be introduced so he can sum things up and hint at the escapades the group gets into.

HOUSE OF STAIRS. William Sleator. Dutton, 1985, 176p., $14.95. JH, HS. Eng, Govt, Psych. Thoughtful; science fiction.

SUBJECT AREAS
Psychology; Friendship; Survival; Self-knowledge; Peer pressure.

CHARACTERS
Peter: the first person to arrive in the house of stairs. He is fearful, quiet, and shy.

Lola: the second person to arrive in the house. She is assertive and rebellious.

Blossom: an overweight and selfish girl. She is the one who finds the food machine.

Abigail: a pretty, delicate girl who goes along with what the others want.

Oliver: a handsome, confident, and energetic boy who becomes the group's leader.

BOOKTALK

Imagine that you are in a place made up entirely of stairs. There are no floors, no ceilings, no walls. Everywhere you look, all you can see are stairs connected by small landings and narrow bridges. If you try to go too far in any direction, the stairs begin turning back on themselves, and you realize that you are trapped— trapped in a house of stairs.

This is the situation five teenagers find themselves in. They discover that they are all 16, all orphans, and all wards of the state. They have no idea where they are, how they got there, or why they are there. Lola finds a place where there is always water. Blossom finds the food machine and learns how to make it work, but they soon realize that they have to cooperate in order to eat. The machine only produces food if they each do certain things at the same time. It's never enough to fill them up, but it's enough to keep them from starving. Obviously whoever put them here wants them to live. But why are they here? The house doesn't give them any answers.

Then one morning the machine won't give them any food no matter what they do. Soon they begin to fight—and immediately the machine gives them food, more than ever before. That's when Lola realizes what the machine is training them to do. Soon they will have to hurt each other, maybe even kill each other, in order to get food.

Can any of them survive?

(Adapted from a talk by Joni Richards Bodart in *Booktalk! 3.*)

MAJOR IDEAS OR THEMES

With time and the right circumstances, almost anyone can be conditioned to do almost anything.

Conditioning works even on people who are aware that they are being trained.

Resisting conditioning requires great determination and strength of character.

Rewarding desired behavior produces better results than punishing unwanted behavior.

It is much easier to persuade a group of people to dislike and mistrust one another than it is to persuade them to work together and be friends.

During times of intense stress, people display their most basic characteristics, whether those are positive or negative.

If you strive to be the best that you can be and are true to yourself, you will be able to like yourself and take pride in your actions, whether or not anyone else understands or agrees with what you have done.

BOOK REPORT IDEAS
1. Discuss the major character traits of each of the characters, and show how the conditioning intensified those traits.
2. Discuss the idea of deliberate conditioning and its positive and negative implications. Remember, we are all conditioned in many ways to do many things that are necessary for our survival.
3. Explain how Abigail, Oliver, and Blossom will be able to use their conditioning to accomplish the jobs they have been trained for.
4. Discuss whether reward or punishment is more effective in producing conditioning quickly, basing your arguments upon Lola's comments to Dr. Lawrence and your own experience.
5. Explain what you think might have been the reasons why Sleator wrote this book and what you understand to be the book's main messages to the reader.

BOOKTALK IDEAS
1. Focus your talk on the setting of the experiment—the house of stairs—and the emotions it inspired in each of the members of the group, or on the training that the group was given by the food machine.
2. Using the first person, introduce each of the five characters, having them describe themselves and their own interpretations of their situation.
3. Create a mood with your voice and words to help your audience picture the setting more clearly. Focus on the emotions of each member of the group when they arrived to help you do this.

📖 📖 📖

I KNOW WHAT YOU DID LAST SUMMER. Lois Duncan. Pocket Books, 1986, 198p., $2.95(pb); Little, Brown, 1973, 199p., $14.95. JH, HS. Eng, Psych. Average; mystery, suspense.

SUBJECT AREAS
Friendship; Revenge; Guilt; Death and dying; School; Working.

CHARACTERS
Julie James: a high school senior and former cheerleader who has just been accepted into Smith College.

Barry Cox: a college freshman, fraternity man, and football star. He dates Helen Rivers and is planning to take a trip to Europe during the summer.

Helen Rivers: a high school dropout who does weather reports, spot announcements, and public appearances for a local TV station, where she is known as the Golden Girl.

Ray Bronson: Julie's former boyfriend. He lived in California for a year and has just moved back to town.

Bud: Julie's new boyfriend. A Vietnam veteran, he's older and more serious than she is.

Collie: Helen's new neighbor at her expensive apartment complex and maybe the new man in her life.

BOOKTALK
Ray and Barry were seniors, Julie and Helen were juniors in high school when it happened. They'd had a picnic in the mountains, complete with something to drink and something to smoke. When they were ready to start back, the boys tossed a coin. Barry lost the toss and had to drive. Julie and Ray, who were sitting in the back seat, weren't paying attention to Barry's driving, even though he was going too fast, as he always did. They didn't realize anything was wrong until Helen screamed, and they sat up in time to see the little boy's body sliding across the hood of the car.

Barry didn't even slow down, but he did stop a little later, just long enough for Ray to make an anonymous phone call to the police. Then he made all of them promise not to tell anyone. He was 18, they'd all had beer and grass, so they'd get the book thrown at them, and he would go to jail. He was persuasive, and everyone gave their word. But Julie still felt guilty, and sent a bunch of yellow roses to the little boy's funeral.

But now it's a year later, and Julie gets the first letter. All it says is, "I know what you did last summer." Helen gets a picture of a boy on a bicycle, and Barry gets a mysterious phone call telling him to go to the stadium late at night. When he does, someone shoots him in the back.

Someone knows that they killed the little boy, and now that someone is going to kill them!

(Adapted from a talk by Mary Moore and Joni Richards Bodart in *Booktalk! 3*.)

MAJOR IDEAS OR THEMES
You can't always go back and fix a mistake. Sometimes you just have to live with the consequences.

You cannot escape the consequences of your actions.

You should always try to do what you think is right, even when others pressure you to act differently.

Revenge is not always sweet.

Friends do not force friends to lie for them.

Be true to yourself and to what you believe is right.

BOOK REPORT IDEAS
1. Describe what you would have done if you had been in the back seat of that car with your date. Justify your answer and make sure that it is realistic.
2. Show how each of the four characters coped with their guilt about killing the little boy.
3. If you figured out who the killer was before the last few pages of the book, explain when you figured it out and which clues you used to do it.
4. Discuss your opinion about the realism of the story. That is, could you really get away with a hit-and-run accident? Explain your belief in detail.

BOOKTALK IDEAS
1. Focus on one of the four main characters and tell the story from their point of view.
2. Focus on each of the four main characters and tell the story from each point of view, showing how differently each of them felt about what they had done.
3. What made you want to read this book? Use that as a hook to get someone else interested in reading it.

📖 📖 📖

1 LOVE YOU, STUPID! Harry Mazer. Avon, 1983, 192p., $2.75(pb); Harper & Row, 1981, 192p., $12.89. HS. Eng, Creat Writing. Average; realistic fiction, humor, romance.

SUBJECT AREAS
Sex and sexuality; Friendship; Family relationships; Working; Writing.

CHARACTERS
Marcus Rosenbloom: a 17-year-old who is equally obsessed with writing and with losing his virginity.

Wendy Barrett: a friend of Marcus who is also a virgin.

Alec: Marcus's best friend. Wendy has a crush on him.

Karen: an older woman whom Marcus fantasizes about.

Sally Rosenbloom; Marcus's mother.

Bill: Sally's lover.

Mr. and Mrs. Barrett: Wendy's parents.

BOOKTALK
Marcus is tall, dark, and handsome. Seventeen-years-old, and a high school senior, he's already a budding writer. He loves girls but doesn't date anyone special. His love life is like his writing—all talk and no action. He's nearly a man, and he's been ready for years, but he's never had sex. He can't stop thinking about it. As far as he's concerned, he's on the wrong side of the wall that divides the world's population—between those who *have* and those who *haven't.*

Then he meets Wendy Barrett—again. He and Wendy grew up together, but then she moved away. Now she's moved back. She's different, and Marcus is intrigued. Maybe she's the one, he thinks, just maybe. He helps her find her way around school, hoping she'll help him find his way around her. When she invites him over to her house and asks if he'd like to see her bedroom, Marcus can't believe it. Finally, after all this time! But when he makes a pass at her, she pushes him away. She wants to be friends, good friends, the kind who can say anything to each other. But what about friends who will do anything for each other, Marcus wonders.

Will he and Wendy ever make it over that wall? And when they do, will it be together, or will they each be with somebody else? (Adapted from a talk by Judy Druse in *Booktalk! 3.*)

MAJOR IDEAS OR THEMES
Sex changes a relationship in fundamental ways.

Sex is not the most important thing that can happen between two people.

It's better to live in the real world than to get lost in daydreams.

Friendship takes time and energy. It doesn't just happen.

Friends are often more important than lovers—unless you can have both in one person.

It's hard to be either a friend or a lover if you aren't willing to talk about your true feelings, even if doing so makes you uncomfortable.

Sometimes love arrives when you least expect it.

BOOK REPORT IDEAS
1. Discuss whether you think this book is realistic and explain why or why not.
2. Look at the role of imagination in this story and show how it both helped and hindered Marcus's and Wendy's relationships, both with each other and with Karen and Alec.
3. Discuss how Marcus and Wendy communicated before and after they became lovers, using examples from the book. Explain why you think their communication patterns changed and whether that change could or should have been avoided.
4. The author used humor to present many ideas in this book. Explain why you think he did and how the book would have been different if he had presented the actions in the book in a nonhumorous fashion.

BOOKTALK IDEAS
1. Use quotes from Marcus's daydreams to tell the story in the first person.
2. Do a character description booktalk, describing Marcus and Wendy in detail and leading up to the scene in Wendy's bedroom when she rejects his first pass.
3. Have Wendy and Marcus take turns describing themselves, each other, and their situation.

INVINCIBLE SUMMER. Jean Ferris. Avon, 1989, 176p., $2.95(pb). HS. Eng, Sociology, Psych. Thoughtful; realistic fiction, romance.

SUBJECT AREAS
Death and dying; Family relationships; Friendship.

CHARACTERS

Robin Gregory: a 17-year-old girl who learns that she has leukemia.

Rick Winn: another leukemia patient who helps Robin deal with her own illness.

Libby Clayton: Robin's grandmother.

Bill Gregory: Robin's father, who runs a small farm.

Marci: Robin's best friend.

Bobby: Marci's boyfriend.

Ivan: Robin's boyfriend before she becomes ill.

BOOKTALK

I first met Rick in the hospital, when I was having tests and he was having chemotherapy. He was nothing like the guys I'd grown up with. They were farm boys whose only interests in life were fun and games and sex. I had more fun sitting next to Rick on a cheap plastic couch in the hospital recreation room and watching a rerun of *Casablanca* than I'd had with any of the guys I'd dated. Rick was different in another way, too. He had leukemia, the same kind that the tests showed I had.

Would I have made it through the next year without Rick? Maybe, but then again maybe not. I know I wouldn't have felt as loved, and I would have never, ever laughed. No one else understood what I was going through the way he did. No one else had his positive attitude, his joy in life, and his certainty that we would both make it through. And no one else loved me the way he did.

"In the depths of winter, I finally learned that within me there lay an invincible summer." This is the story of ours.
(Adapted from a talk by Joni Richards Bodart in *Booktalk! 3.* Quote is from Camus.)

MAJOR IDEAS OR THEMES

Love can outlast death.

Joy in life is what makes it worth living.

Facing the inevitability of death makes even the little things in life seem more precious.

If you have had a particular experience, you are more able to empathize with someone who is going through the same thing.

Sometimes a loved one's pain makes us want to turn away, even when it is not the most loving thing to do.

Death is not the worst thing that can happen to someone—even though it may seem to be.

BOOK REPORT IDEAS
1. Describe why Robin and Rick were drawn together so quickly.
2. Compare the ways Robin's family helped her with the way Rick's family treated him.
3. Explain why Robin's friends stopped coming to see her. How did she feel about that?
4. Show what gave Rick the strength and the faith he had in life.
5. Show how Rick and Robin supported each other.
6. Compare Robin's philosophy at the beginning and the end of the book. How had it changed and how had it stayed the same?
7. Describe how the idea of love outlasting death is portrayed in the book.

BOOKTALK IDEAS
1. Tell the story from Rick's point of view rather than from Robin's.
2. Have each of them describe each other and how they met and learned that they had the same disease.
3. Describe how even the details of life became important when Rick and Robin learned that they had cancer.

LANGUAGE OF GOLDFISH. Zibby Oneal. Penguin, 1990, 190p., $3.95(pb); Viking, 1980, 179p., $14.95. HS. Eng, Psych, Art. Thoughtful; realistic fiction.

SUBJECT AREAS
Death and dying; Suicide; Mental illness; Family relationships; Self-knowledge; Friendship; Art.

CHARACTERS
Carrie Stokes: a teenager who seems to have everything that she could want.

Moira Stokes: Carrie's older sister.

Dr. Ross: the psychiatrist who helps Carrie understand why she feels crazy and how to get well.

Mr. and Mrs. Stokes: Carrie's parents, who refuse to admit that anything is wrong with her.

Sophie: the Stokes's maid.

Duncan Stokes: Carrie's little brother.

Mrs. Ramsey: Carrie's art teacher.

Matt and Daniel Spangler: the Stokes's new next-door neighbors.

BOOKTALK

It began with a dizzy spell and a kaleidoscope of tumbling colors, and gradually it started to take over her life. One day, on the way to her little brother's hockey game, Carrie blacked out. When she woke up she was on the very edge of town, with no memory of how she got there. She'd lost over two hours of her life, but neither her parents nor her sister listened when she told them she was going crazy.

Desperate to get their attention, Carrie swallowed a whole bottle of pills and ended up in the hospital, only to discover that her suicide attempt had been a failure. Her mother was sure it was all an accident. It wasn't until Carrie made a scene, screaming and throwing things, that she was finally able to get some help.

But not even Dr. Ross could tell her what was wrong. He could only help her find out for herself. Would she be able to figure out what was wrong and what to do about it before her fears and obsessions overwhelmed her, or would she be stuck in limbo, less a part of the world around her than of the frightening world inside her head?

MAJOR IDEAS OR THEMES

Change is inevitable, so each of us must learn to live with it.

Psychiatrists don't cure patients; they help them learn how to cure themselves.

Friendship means accepting both the good and the bad parts of someone else.

You can only cover up inner turmoil so long before it breaks out.

Sometimes you have to shout to get people's attention and show them you are in pain.

Art is an expression of who the artist is. As the person changes, so does the art.

Suicide attempts are often a cry for help, rather than an attempt to end everything.

The strength you need to survive can only come from inside yourself.

BOOK REPORT IDEAS

1. Carrie's art changed as she became sicker and then again as she began to get well. Trace the changes and show how they reflected what was going on in her mind.
2. Discuss the response of Carrie's family to her illness and their unwillingness to deal with it. How do you think their actions affected Carrie both as she got sick and as she got well?
3. Examine Dr. Ross's role in the book and the way he reacted to Carrie during their sessions.
4. Evaluate the actions of the characters in the book, especially Carrie, and show how you think they were realistic or unrealistic.

BOOKTALK IDEAS

1. Illustrate your talk with a picture that might have been one of Carrie's and/or with one of the Beardsley prints that were referred to in the book.
2. Introduce Carrie from several different points of view—Moira's, her parents', Mrs. Ramsey's, and Dr. Ross's.
3. Using a plot summary technique, focus on Carrie's increasing illness, leading up to her suicide attempt.
4. Using a mood-based technique, and speaking in the first person as Carrie, try to create in your audience an understanding of the way Carrie felt as she got sicker and sicker and no one would listen to her. You might want to use illustrations in this talk as suggested in number 1 above.

📖 📖 📖

THE LAST MISSION. Harry Mazer. Dell, 1981, 188p., $3.25(pb). HS. Am Hist, Eng, Psych. Thoughtful; historical fiction, adventure.

SUBJECT AREAS

War; Runaways; Self-knowledge; Friendship; Family relationships; Courage; Working; Death and dying; Other countries/Europe; Survival.

CHARACTERS

Jack Raab: a 15-year-old who steals his brother's birth certificate so he can join the Army. He becomes the waist gunner on a bomber called Godfathers, Inc.

Irving Raab: Jack's older brother, who failed the medical exam for the military.

Gary Martin: the pilot of Godfathers, Inc.

Milt Held: the co-pilot.

Sam Seppetone: the navigator.

Paul Johnson: the tail gunner.

Chuckie O'Brien: the radio operator and Jack's best friend.

Fred Pratt: the nose gunner.

Dave Gonzalez: the bail-turret gunner.

Billy Eustice: the flight engineer.

Dotty Landon: a girl whom Jack meets at the end of basic training.

Stan Wakowski: a soldier whom Jack meets in a German hospital.

Willy and Karl: German guards who befriend Jack and Stan and promise to take them to the American lines.

BOOKTALK

Jack Raab was big for his 15 years, so no one suspected anything when he used his older brother's birth certificate to lie about his age and enlist in the Army Air Corps. It was 1944, and he was anxious to be in the middle of the action. When he got there, though, he discovered the truth in the old saying, "War is hell."

Being a waist gunner in a bomber flying missions over Germany was not the fun he had expected it to be. He soon realized that the bullets were real and that they killed people. He killed people. War wasn't for heroes—it was a job, a job that you had to do whether you liked it or not.

Then the plane was shot down and Jack ended up alone behind enemy lines, haunted by memories of the broken bodies of his friends and crewmates. Only then did it begin to sink in just how hellish war can be, especially when you're only 15 years old.

MAJOR IDEAS OR THEMES

War is not the best way to solve conflicts.

People can grow up fast when they have to.

Eventually the truth always comes out.

You can't go home again, at least not to the home you left behind, because it and you will have changed.

BOOK REPORT IDEAS

1. Compare the person Jack was when he entered the army and when he was discharged, describing how and why he had changed.
2. Discuss the idea "You can't go home again," and show how Jack discovered that it is true.
3. Jack's ideas about war changed greatly during the time he was in the Air Corps. Explain how your ideas about war have changed recently, based not only on this book but also on recent world events and how they have affected your beliefs and philosophies.

BOOKTALK IDEAS

1. Write a plot summary booktalk, leading up to either the mission when the plane had to be ditched or the last mission.
2. Write the talk as if you were Chuckie describing Jack and their friendship.
3. Compare Jack's experiences in the military with the experiences of more modern soldiers fighting in Vietnam or in the Persian Gulf.
4. Write the talk as if it were a speech that Jack was making to your class about his experiences. This talk would be most effective in the first person.

📖 📖 📖

MANIAC MAGEE. Jerry Spinelli. Little, Brown, 1990, 184p., $13.95. JH, HS. Eng, Am Hist. Average; realistic fiction, humor.

SUBJECT AREAS

Runaways; Blacks; Self-knowledge; Homeless people; Survival; Friendship; Love; Rites of passage; Racism; Peer pressure.

CHARACTERS

Jeffrey Lionel (Maniac) Magee: a boy who becomes a legend in his own time, because he does what no other kid dares to do.

Amanda Beale: a black girl who is the first person to talk to Maniac when he arrives in Two Mills.

Brian Denehy and James "Hands" Down: two members of the East End high school football team.

John McNab: a white kid who pitches a frogball to Maniac.

Mars Bar Thompson: the first black kid to challenge Maniac.

Mrs. Beale: Amanda's mother, who gives Maniac his first home in Two Mills.

Grayson: an ex-ballplayer who rescues Maniac from the buffalo pen at the zoo.

Russell and Piper McNab: John's little brothers.

BOOKTALK

Maniac wasn't his real name, but that's what everyone called him, because he did what no other kid would dare to do, and got away with it. He lived with a family in the East End when only black families lived there. He went into the Fisterwalds' backyard to rescue Arnold Jones, when no kid from the white West End would even deliver papers to their house.

Maniac knew how to do a lot of things, like how to run down the railroad tracks on the rail, not the ties, how to untie the hardest knots, how to hit the fastest softball pitch, and how to throw the longest passes. In one sense, though, he was blind. He couldn't see why folks in the East End didn't like him, and he couldn't see what the big deal was about whether someone was black or white. He didn't see any black people in the East End. He saw dark fudge and light fudge and gingersnap and acorn and butter rum and burnt orange, but he never saw anyone who was licorice, which is black. When he looked at his own body, he saw six or seven different colors. The only part that was white was his eyeballs, just like everyone else's.

Most of all, Maniac didn't see that some kids don't like other kids who aren't like them. They don't like kids who don't watch TV on Saturday morning, who do the dishes without being told, who are allergic to pizza, and who show them up and make them look bad—especially if that kid is a different color. That's why folks remember Maniac, because he did what no one else would for the kids of the East End and the kids of the West End—and that's a pretty good way to be remembered.

MAJOR IDEAS OR THEMES

People are people, regardless of the color of their skin.

Sometimes it is better to walk away rather than let someone you love get hurt.

People are more likely to believe what you show them than what you tell them.

Home is the place that when you go there, they won't turn you away.

Sometimes kids can see what adults cannot.

An outsider can sometimes see what is happening more clearly than an insider can.

Love is color-blind.

Even being a hero doesn't make a difference if someone doesn't like what color your skin is.

BOOK REPORT IDEAS
1. Discuss the character of Maniac Magee, showing why he was who he was and why the kids paid attention to what he did.
2. Describe Maniac's most unusual characteristics. Explain why you think he had those characteristics and why you think people reacted to them and to him the way they did.
3. While there are not many adults in this book, they had a different view of Maniac than the kids did. Describe their view of him and show how it had an effect on the way the kids saw him.
4. Speculate on what you think happened to Maniac after the end of this book. If you were to write a sequel to it, how old would Maniac be and what would he be doing? Be sure to also bring the lives of the other main characters up-to-date unless by the time your sequel takes place, Maniac has left Two Mills and doesn't have any contact with any of the characters in the book.
5. Discuss what you believe is the most important lesson in this book and why the author wrote it. What was Maniac's heritage, his monument?
6. By the end of the book, Maniac has made two friends, Amanda and Mars Bar. Amanda had been on his side from the beginning, but Mars Bar wasn't. Explain the events or series of events that you think caused him to change his mind and become Maniac's friend.

BOOKTALK IDEAS
1. Use the jump-rope rhyme as part of your talk.
2. Include a list of Maniac's exploits as part of your talk.
3. Maniac didn't talk much about himself, so let several kids from both the West End and the East End introduce him to the audience in your talk, giving their own views of him.

🕮 🕮 🕮

MISSING SINCE MONDAY. Ann Martin. Scholastic, 1988, 176p., $2.50(pb); Holiday House, 1986, 176p., $12.50. JH, HS. Eng. Quick read; realistic fiction, mystery, romance.

SUBJECT AREAS
Stepparents; Kidnapping; Family relationships; Mental illness; Friendship.

CHARACTERS
Maggie Ellis: a high school sophomore whose little sister is kidnapped while she is in Maggie's care.

Mike Ellis: Maggie's brother and a high school senior.

Courtenay Ellis: Maggie and Mike's half-sister. She is a bright and trusting 4-year-old.

Leigh Ellis: Courtenay's mother and Mike and Maggie's stepmother.

Owen Ellis: the children's father and Leigh's husband.

David Jacobssen: Maggie's boyfriend and Mike's friend.

Martha Jacobssen: David's twin sister and Maggie's best friend.

Andrew de Christopher: Mike's best friend.

Jane de Christopher: Martha and Maggie's friend.

Brad de Christopher: Andrew and Jane's older brother. He's a strange person whom Jane avoids.

Jessica Ellis: Mike and Maggie's mother, whom they haven't seen in years.

BOOKTALK
I couldn't believe it. My little sister, Courtenay, was gone—kidnapped! Mike and I had been in charge of her while our parents were in the Caribbean, and that morning we'd gotten her ready for school, seen her onto the school bus, and gone on to school ourselves. When the bus didn't drop her off after school, I called the school to see what the problem was. The last thing I expected to hear was that she'd never made it to school. The bus driver—Courtie's favorite one—had dropped her off with the rest of the kids. The others had been at school all day, but no one had seen Courtie.

After that everything moved like a dream—or a nightmare. But it was all too real. The police came and questioned us and took some pictures we had of her to help them in the search. When Mike finally got through to Dad and Leigh, Leigh directed all her anger at me. She almost seemed to think I'd lost Courtie on purpose. And then there were the things Dad said when the police officer asked him why he and our mother had gotten divorced. Suddenly I discovered that all of the things he'd been saying about her for years were lies, lies he said were to protect Mike and me. Only now they didn't seem like protection at all.

Then there were the phone calls, more weird calls like the ones I'd been getting for a couple of weeks before Courtie disappeared. When the caller mentioned her, I got really scared. Could he be the one who had kidnapped her, and if he had, would I be next?

MAJOR IDEAS OR THEMES

People are not always what they seem, nor are our memories of them always accurate.

Telling lies to protect someone may actually end up hurting them when the truth finally comes out.

It is better to prepare children for the dangers in the world outside their home than to try to protect them by pretending that the dangers don't exist.

Unpleasant as the truth may be, it is better to look it in the face and deal with it than to ignore it or pretend it isn't so.

Sometimes tragedy can help people change and grow closer together.

BOOK REPORT IDEAS

1. Because of Courtie's disappearance, everyone in the family changed the way they thought of themselves and each other. Describe those changes, showing why and how they took place.
2. Show the ways that Maggie and Mike acted responsibly while they were in charge of Courtie and after she disappeared. If you see other things they could have done to protect their little sister, explain them in detail.
3. Explain why you think the character of Jessica, including her relationship with Maggie and Mike, was or was not realistic, giving details from the book to support your theory. Discuss the scenes that foreshadowed or predicted the final ending by describing Jessica, her actions, or ethers' views of her.
4. Compare the characters of Jessica and Leigh as mother figures.

BOOKTALK IDEAS

1. Tell the booktalk in the first person as if you were Maggie or Mike.
2. Focus your talk on the scene when Maggie discovers that Courtie is missing, beginning with her growing sense of unease as she waits for the bus.
3. Introduce your talk with statistics about the number of children that disappear every year. Consider using a milk carton or some other item with a picture of a lost child as a prop for your talk. (This would be especially effective if that child resembled Courtie.)

4. How would you feel if a member of your family disappeared? Remember, it is one thing to talk about such a thing and quite another to deal with the reality of the event. Use your own emotions to help you understand and explain the emotions of the characters in the book.

📖 📖 📖

NELL'S QUILT. Susan Terris. Scholastic, 1988, 176p., $2.50 (pb); FSG, 1987. 192p., $12.95. JH, HS. Am Hist, Psych, Eng. Quick read; historical fiction.

SUBJECT AREAS
Eating disorders; Family relationships; Self-knowledge; Suicide.

CHARACTERS
Nell Edmonds: an 18-year-old whose parents urge her to marry although she wants to attend college.

Eliza Edmonds: Nell's sister. She is 17 and frail from a bout with rheumatic fever.

Papa: an overworked farmer who barely makes enough to support his family.

Mama: a woman nearly broken by hard work who has little sympathy for her daughter's dreams.

Rob Hoffman: Nell's best friend from a nearby farm. He hopes Nell will marry him.

Anson Tanner: a widower whom Nell's parents want her to marry.

Jewel Tanner: Anson's young daughter.

Tobias: the Hoffmans' new hired man.

BOOKTALK
When Nell's parents announced that she was going to marry Anson Tanner, she knew that her dream of going to college would never become a reality. Ever since she could remember, her parents had controlled every aspect of her life, and it was obvious they intended to go on doing it. She could see no way out.

At first, making a crazy quilt was just a way to avoid having to talk with her future husband, as well as a way to hide her anger at her own helplessness. Gradually, however, Nell began to realize that she did have some control. She could control the patterns she made in the quilt, and she could control the amount of food she allowed herself to eat.

Day by day, the quilt grew larger and more beautiful. And day by day, Nell grew thinner. Would she, by the time the quilt was finished, succeed in thwarting her family's plans for her? Would she finally take control of her life by starving herself to death?

MAJOR IDEAS OR THEMES
When you have no control over your own life, you may feel that it is not worth living.

People will go to great lengths, even as far as killing themselves, in order to have some control over their lives.

The behavior of one family member effects every other member.

Parents are often not aware of the effects their words and actions have upon their children.

Children must be allowed to make some of their own decisions in order to have a feeling of worth and power.

BOOK REPORT IDEAS
1. Discuss how Nell begins to realize she does have some control in her life.
2. Detail some of the other things Nell might have done to establish control. Be sure to stay within the historical context of the story.
3. Relate this story to modern stories of eating disorders.
4. Discuss the importance of power in an individual's life using examples from this and other books.

BOOKTALK IDEAS
1. Tell the story as if you were Nell.
2. Talk about the likenesses and differences between this story set in the 1800s and stories about anorexia nervosa set in the present.
3. Talk about each of the characters and how they related to Nell or how she saw them.

📖 📖 📖

THE OUTSIDERS S. E. Hinton. Dell, 1968, 156p., $3.25(pb); Viking, 1967, 188p., $12.95. JH, HS. Eng, Sociology. Average; realistic fiction.

SUBJECT AREAS
Family relationships; Friendship; Death and dying; Social prejudice; Gangs; Peer pressure.

CHARACTERS
The Greasers
Ponyboy Curtis: a 14-year-old orphan who lives with his two older brothers.

Sodapop Curtis: Ponyboy's favorite brother. He is 16, a high school dropout who works as a mechanic.

Darry Curtis: Ponyboy's 20-year-old brother, who turned down a college scholarship and took a job in order to support his younger brothers.

Two-Bit Mathews: an 18-year-old shoplifter who thinks life is a joke.

Steve Randle: Sodapop's best friend, a smart, cocky 17-year-old who is good at fixing—and stealing—cars.

Dallas Winston: the toughest, coldest, and meanest Greaser.

Johnny Cade: Ponyboy's friend, a smallish 16-year-old who is the gang's "pet."

The Socs
Cherry Valance: a pretty, sensitive, and friendly cheerleader.

Marcia: Cherry's friend. She has a wacky sense of humor.

Bob: Cherry's boyfriend, who likes to party and to fight.

Randy: Bob's best friend.

BOOKTALK
Ponyboy is a Greaser from the wrong side of town. He has long hair and sometimes carries a switchblade. But he's also a dreamer who likes books, movies, and sunsets. His parents are dead, and he lives with his older brothers, Darry and Sodapop. Their only friends are the boys in their gang: Dallas, wild, restless, and hard; Steve, who specializes in stealing cars as well as fixing them; Two-Bit, famous for his wisecracks and his long, black switchblade; and Johnny, who looks a little like a small, dark puppy lost in a crowd. The Greasers' biggest rivals are the Socs, rich kids who wear madras and drive Mustangs. Johnny is the gentlest and most vulnerable member of the gang, but he is the one the Socs choose to beat up one night when they find him

alone. After that, he carries a huge switchblade and vows that he'll use it on the next Soc who tries anything with him.

It isn't long before Johnny and Ponyboy come across the same gang of Socs, reeling drunk and in a nasty mood. When they try to drown Ponyboy, Johnny gets a chance to use his switchblade. He and Ponyboy get away just ahead of the police.

The Outsiders is Ponyboy's story of what happened after that night.

(Adapted from a talk by Joni Richards Bodart in *Booktalk! 3*.)

MAJOR IDEAS OR THEMES
Be true to yourself and your beliefs.

In order to see people as they really are, we must look beyond appearances and social class.

Those we love live on in our hearts and minds even after their deaths.

Life is not fair, but that does not mean it is not worth living.

Love is expressed in many ways, some of which may not fit our usual interpretations of love.

A family is a group of people who love each other and who stick together in spite of what happens. It does not have to be a biological family.

Even though they may fight among themselves, family members will unite against threats from the outside.

BOOK REPORT IDEAS
1. Explain the meaning of the phrase "stay gold."
2. Ponyboy decides to write his semester theme about his gang for some very specific reasons. List those reasons and show why he thought they were important. Do you agree with his reasons? Why or why not?
3. Speculate on what you think will happen when Cherry sees Ponyboy at school. Do you think she will talk to him? Why or why not?
4. Discuss what is, in your opinion, the most important part of this book. Explain why you feel this way.
5. Describe what you think happened after the end of the book. Give character descriptions of each of the gang members, in five years and in ten years. If any are dead, include the way that they died.
6. Decide which group you would rather be part of, the Greasers or the Socs and explain why.
7. Show how the members of the gang were like a family and explain why the gang was important to them. What are some other groups that could have taken the place of the gang in their lives?

BOOKTALK IDEAS
1. Tell the story from Johnny's or Cherry's point of view.
2. Use Ponyboy's own words to tell the story, with excerpts from the book.
3. Describe each of the Greasers and the Socs, then in just a few sentences, set up the reasons why they were fighting.

THE PIGMAN. Paul Zindel. Bantam, 1983, 176p., $3.50(pb); Harper & Row, 1968, 192p., $13.95. JH. Eng. Average; realistic fiction.

SUBJECT AREAS
Friendship; Aging; Self-knowledge; Death and dying; Crime and delinquency; Family relationships; Love; Rites of passage; Peer pressure.

CHARACTERS
John Conlon: a high school sophomore who hates school and loves practical jokes.

Lorraine Jensen: John's best friend and his phone game partner.

Norton Kelly: a student who doesn't like John but who still plays phone games with him.

Dennis Korbin: another student who joins in the phone games.

Angelo Pignati: the Pigman, an old and lonely man whom John and Lorraine meet while playing phone games.

BOOKTALK
No matter what anyone says, we never meant to hurt the Pigman. It's important that everyone know that, so we've decided to write down the whole story of what happened between us and the Pigman, and we agree to tell the whole truth, every bit of it, even when it hurts.

It all started with telephone marathon. That's when you pick a number out of the phone book and try to get whoever answers the phone to talk as long as you can. I'm Lorraine, and I was the one who chose the Pigman's number. But it was John who said we should go see him and get the donation he promised to give us for the phony charity we said we were representing.

If only we had stopped there, all the bad things would never have happened. But we didn't, and somehow one thing led to another—and now everything is different, and it won't ever be the same again. We won't ever be the same again.

But please don't let anyone tell you that we're juvenile delinquents, or that we planned what happened from the start. We didn't. It just happened—and now we have to live with the consequences of what we did. But we never meant to hurt anyone, really!

MAJOR IDEAS OR THEMES
Anyone can be lonely, no matter how old they are.

When it comes to parent-child misunderstandings, being too much alike can cause as many problems as being very different.

Small mistakes can have far-reaching consequences.

Good intentions aren't always enough, and sometimes they can backfire, causing even more problems.

Sometimes it isn't enough to say you're sorry.

Betrayal hurts both the betrayer and the one betrayed.

You can't change what has already happened, no matter how much you want to.

BOOK REPORT IDEAS
1. People become friends partly because of what they have in common with each other. Describe what John, Lorraine, and the Pigman had in common that made them such good friends.
2. Discuss your understanding of why the party took place after John and Lorraine had spent so much time cleaning up, including why you think it got out of hand so quickly. What is the underlying meaning to this part of the story?
3. Describe the relationship John and Lorraine had with their parents and how that relationship affected the rest of their lives.
4. Discuss what you learned from this book and which part or parts of it you think you will remember most clearly. Include why you think the author wrote it and what he was trying to say to the reader.

BOOKTALK IDEAS
1. Write your talk from both John's and Lorraine's points of view, just as the book is written, letting each of them tell part of the story.
2. Use a small statue of a pig to illustrate your report—perhaps one like one of the Pigman's.
3. Write part of your talk from the Pigman's point of view as he describes John and Lorraine and his friendship with them.

◫ ◫ ◫

PLAGUE YEAR. Stephanie Tolan. Fawcett, 1991, 185p., $3.99(pb); Morrow, 1989, 208p., $12.95. HS. Eng, Soc Studies. Average; realistic fiction.

SUBJECT AREAS
Secrets; Crime and delinquency; Death and dying; Prejudice; School; Self-knowledge; Friendship; Family relationships; Child abuse; Rites of passage.

CHARACTERS
David Watson: a runner and loner who tries to befriend Bran.

Molly Pepper: an independent girl who is the first to make friends with Bran.

Bran Slocam: a newcomer who stands out because of his ponytail, gold earring, and wild eye.

Nick Bruno: a loud, obnoxious bully who is determined to get a reaction from Bran.

Kristin Mattis: the cheerleader whom David is dating.

Matt Singleton, Jerry Ritoni, and Gordon Krosky: friends of Nick's who join him in tormenting Bran.

James Watson: David's father, a woodcarver.

Dr. Towson: the high school principal.

Mr. Byrd: the contemporary social issues teacher. He defends Bran before the whole town.

Mr. and Mrs. Ridley: Bran's uncle and aunt.

Angela Ridley: Bran's cousin and the twins' mother.

Zach Lewis: a reporter on the school newspaper who tries to interview Bran.

Jeremy Collier: Bran's father, a convicted serial killer.

BOOKTALK
Molly called what happened that October a plague, but I'm not all that sure she was right. A plague comes from outside and infects people. What happened here wasn't something from outside, it

was something that was inside the people here, or most of them. It was surely inside Molly and me.

It all started the day Bran Slocum came to town. He looked different, with his ponytail and gold earring, and he acted different, never reacting to any of the taunts or tricks Nick and his gang played on him, always quiet and always alone. Then the reporter came to town with a story about the son of a serial killer going to our school, and the description fit Bran like a glove. It was all over town right away, and the ugly side of people I'd known all my life began to show. They said he was a bad seed, that he'd start killing kids like his father did. That wasn't true. Molly and I were the only ones who really knew him. We knew how gentle he was, how great he was with his twin nephews, and how much he loved them.

Maybe if I'd done something more it would've made a difference, or maybe Molly was right and nothing could have changed anything. This plague didn't have a cure. All I know now is that I don't like this town as much as I used to, now that I've seen what lies behind those smiles and kind words. It's changed, and it'll never be the same—and neither will I.

MAJOR IDEAS OR THEMES

Sometimes it's best to let people keep their secrets.

Some people enjoy hurting those they see as weaker than themselves.

Standing out in a crowd can be dangerous.

Sometimes not responding to violence can incite even more violence, just as an angry response can.

Standing up for the underdog may mean that you will also be persecuted.

Those who spend their time hurting others may find that no one is around when they themselves need help.

Some secrets can destroy friendships.

BOOK REPORT IDEAS

1. There are a number of killers in this book other than Joseph Collier, and they, like him, seemed normal most of the time. Identify these people and explain why you selected them.
2. There are several instances of irony in this book, one of which is the fact that Bran chose to look so different because his father looked so conventional. Discuss some of the other instances of irony you found.
3. Molly said what happened to the town when Bran arrived was like a plague and that nothing could have stopped it. Take a stand

and agree or disagree with that view, citing incidents from the book to support your argument.

4. Bran was quiet and didn't respond violently to anything anyone did to him. Discuss how that was or was not a result of his father's actions and what he might have been like before his father was arrested.

5. Discuss the final scene at the quarry and the actions of each person involved. For instance, why did Bran show himself and take on Nick and his gang when he had not responded violently before?

6. Explain what this book says to you and what you felt the most powerful or memorable part of it was for you. What will you take away with you from this book, and what do you think you will not be able to forget about it?

BOOKTALK IDEAS

1. Use the idea of the plague in your talk and how anger and hatred spread from Nick and his gang to the whole town.

2. Make Bran the focus of your talk using a character description technique.

3. Use the idea of secrets in your talk, the one that Bran had, the secret darker side of the town, and hinting at the one that Molly and David share at the end of the book.

📖 📖 📖

PLAYING BEATIE BOW. Ruth Park. Penguin, 1984, 200p., $3.95(pb); Macmillan, 1982, 204p., $13.95. JH, HS. Hist, Eng. Average; historical fiction, adventure, romance, fantasy.

SUBJECT AREAS

Time travel; Family relationships Historical fiction; Rites of passage; Self-knowledge; Love.

CHARACTERS

Abigail Kirk: a 14-year-old who lives with her divorced mother in Sydney, Australia.

Kathy Kirk: Abigail's mother, a successful businesswoman.

Natalie and Vincent Crown: the Kirks's next-door neighbors.

Weyland Kirk: Abigail's father, a well-known architect.

Beatie Bow: an 11-year-old girl who travels to the present from her home in New South Wales in the 1870s. When she returns she accidentally brings Abigail with her.

Granny: Beatie's grandmother, who believes Abigail is the answer to a prophecy.

Judah: Beatie's older brother, a seaman.

Dovey: Beatie's cousin, who is to marry Judah.

Gibbie: Beatie's sickly 9-year-old brother.

Samuel Bow: Judah, Beatie, and Gibbie's father, a retired soldier.

BOOKTALK
One minute Abigail was a perfectly normal 14-year-old, even if she didn't have any real friends and wore odd-looking clothes she made herself. The next minute she had followed the strange little girl off the playground and into the previous century. Now she was stuck in the year 1873, when the queen's name was Victoria instead of Elizabeth, and people were kinder than people in her own time, although their lives seemed harder.

The only person who knew how Abigail could get back to her own time refused to tell her, until Abigail had fulfilled a prophecy by doing a task that only she could do. The problem was that no one, least of all Abigail, knew what that task was. It was only after she had grown to love the family that had taken her in and fallen in love for the first time that Abigail discovered what she had to do in order to go home.
(Adapted from a talk by Linda Lapides in *Booktalk! 2.*)

MAJOR IDEAS OR THEMES
Goodness will be rewarded.

Love conquers all.

People of other times were not that much different from people who are living today.

Parents make mistakes just like anyone else.

The more you know about people or situations, the easier it is to understand them.

Knowledge can lead to understanding and forgiveness.

BOOK REPORT IDEAS

1. Describe how and why Abigail changed while she was in the past. Contrast how Abigail saw herself and her family on the day she went into the past and on the day she returned.
2. Explain what you think is the most important thing Abigail learned in the past. Then explain the most important thing you learned from her travels.
3. Describe how you felt about the ending. If you didn't like it, how would you have ended the book?
4. Look at some of the differences between daily life in 1873 and today.
5. Pretend you could go into the past and describe when and where you'd go, what you would do when you got there, and why you chose that time and place.

BOOKTALK IDEAS

1. Tell Abigail's story in the first person, as she must have lived it, describing what she saw as she went into the past, building up suspense, and not revealing that she has traveled in time until the last sentence.
2. Tell Beatie's story, describing the modern world as she saw it.

📖 📖 📖

REMEMBERING THE GOOD TIMES. Richard Peck. Dell, 1986, 181p., $2.95(pb); Delacorte, 1985, 192p., $14.95. HS. Eng, Psych. Thoughtful; realistic fiction.

SUBJECT AREAS

Death and dying; Suicide; Friendship; Family relationships; School; Self-knowledge; Rites of passage.

CHARACTERS

Buck Mendenhall: a boy who lives with his father in an old trailer behind a gas station.

Trav Kirby: a brilliant, handsome teenager who is unhappy despite his material advantages.

Kate Lucas: a slender, pretty girl who's the leader of the trio of friends—Buck, Trav, and herself.

Mr. and Mrs. Kirby: Trav's parents, who love him but don't understand him.

Irene and Scotty: the couple who owns the gas station near Buck's trailer.

Polly Prior: Kate's ancient and feisty great-grandmother, who loves to cheat at cards.

Dad: Buck's father, who spends time with him and trusts him.

Skeeter Calhoun: a bully who has a grudge against Buck.

Rusty Hazenfield: a Californian with wild clothes and a flamboyant personality. She joins the trio for a while.

BOOKTALK

They were three friends, Kate, Buck, and Trav. Their friendship started in eighth grade and carried over into high school. Three friends as close as anyone could be. They spent all their time together and really didn't care for anyone's company but their own. They were a kind of family. Buck's parents were divorced and he lived with his dad. Kate had never known her father, and her mother was almost more of a child than she was. Trav lived with his parents, but he couldn't talk to them—the gap between them was too wide for him to bridge. But Trav, Kate, and Buck had each other, and it was good.

Sure, they had their problems on and off, but mostly everything was easy. They all knew everything about each other and understood each other. After all, they were best friends.

Three friends, but suddenly there were only two. Two left wondering why and feeling like they should have seen the signs and done something to help. But they hadn't known—their best friend, and they hadn't known.

How well do you know your best friend?

(Adapted from a talk by Melinda Waugh in *Booktalk! 3.*)

MAJOR IDEAS OR THEMES

Your memories of the people you have loved will keep them alive in your heart.

Suicide not only takes a life, it also damages the people left behind, who must cope with their guilt and pain and the fact that their lives are changed and diminished forever.

No matter how well we think we know someone, there may always be a part of them that is private, secret, and alone.

Sometimes even the support of friends is not enough to overcome a person's private emptiness.

Crying for someone you have lost does not bring them back, but it can help you grieve and then go on with your own life.

BOOK REPORT IDEAS

1. One reason this book was written was because the author found in talking to teens that suicide was frequently thought of as a viable option to problems that seemed too big to handle. In your experience, is this still true, and if so, why is it true? If it is not true, what things have changed so that it is not?
2. Describe the danger signs that people missed that might have prevented Trav's death.
3. Discuss the scene or section of the book that you feel is the most memorable or involving and explain why you chose that section.
4. Explain how you think this book might help someone considering suicide or someone who had a friend who committed suicide. What message do you think the author was trying to communicate to the reader?
5. This book is about friendship as well as death. Explain what it says to you about both of these subjects.

BOOKTALK IDEAS

1. Using a character description technique, introduce Kate, Buck, and Trav, ending with the hint that soon there will be only two of these friends left to cope alone.
2. Focus your talk on the idea of suicide and on the plot rather than on the characters in the book.
3. Using the first person, speaking as Kate, describe Buck, Trav, their friendship, and their loss. Be sure not to give away who dies.
4. Use an old Paddington Bear as a prop for your talk. This would be especially effective for a talk in which Kate speaks in the first person.
5. Use another of the old toys that Trav had kept or a calculator as a prop for your talk.

RUNNING LOOSE. Chris Crutcher. Dell, 1986, 190p., $2.95(pb); Greenwillow Books, 1983, 160p., $13.95. HS. Eng, PE, Ethics. Thoughtful; realistic fiction.

SUBJECT AREAS

Sports; Self-knowledge; Blacks; Racism; Ethics; Love; Death and dying; Family relationships; Rites of passage; Friendship; Working; Survival; Peer pressure.

CHARACTERS

Louie Banks: a high school senior with a starting position on the football team, good friends, and a terrific girlfriend.

Carter: Louie's best friend, who is also a football player.

Boomer Cowans: a star football player, whom Louie dislikes.

Couch Lednecky: the football coach. He will do anything for a winning season and a championship team.

Mr. Jasper: the high school principal.

Becky Sanders: Louie's girlfriend.

Mr. Sanders: Becky's father, who understands his daughter very well.

Coach Madison: a new coach who doesn't approve of Lednecky's methods.

Norm: Louie's father, who trusts him and stands up for him.

Brenda: Louie's mother, who worries about him. She also stands up for him.

Tracy: Louie's little sister.

Washington: a black football player for a rival school. He is an excellent athlete.

Dakota: the owner of the Buckhorn Bar.

BOOKTALK

Louie Banks thought he had it made. It was his senior year, and he had a car and a starting spot on the football team. His grades were okay, and he was dating Becky Sanders. He figured he could just put it into neutral and cruise on into graduation, no sweat.

He might have been able to do it, too, if everything hadn't fallen apart. It all started when Coach Lednecky told them to take out the new Black player on the other team and he didn't care how. Louie couldn't believe it, and when he saw the player lying there on the ground, he just lost it. He threw down his helmet and walked off the field and off the team. The principal wanted to kick him out of school, too—said he didn't want anyone with Louie's attitude running loose on campus. But he could have survived all that, if only Becky hadn't been in that accident. That was when he really lost it.

Louie learned a lot that year, things he never expected to learn and things he didn't want to learn. He learned that it doesn't pay to be honorable with dishonorable men; that you can get through anything if you have people around you who care; that real friends are worth everything; and that death is vicious and miserable and ugly when it takes someone you love. But there were some things Louie *didn't* learn. He didn't learn to like people who didn't like him, and he didn't learn *not* to push his luck.

(Adapted from a talk by Judy Druse in *Booktalk! 2.*)

MAJOR IDEAS OR THEMES

Some things just happen. There isn't any reason for them, and no one is to blame.

If a game is too simple, with no challenges and no surprises, it's not worth playing.

Trying to act honorably with dishonorable people is usually ineffective.

Friends are people who stick by you no matter what and don't criticize your decisions, even if they disagree with them.

The most important person who can accept you is yourself.

You are responsible for everything you do.

The rules of life don't change as you get older, but it is occasionally necessary to learn additional ones.

BOOK REPORT IDEAS

1. There are a variety of ethical viewpoints in this book. Discuss the contrast between them and how these people demonstrated their ethical beliefs in their lives and actions.
2. Louie learned many things during his senior year. Discuss what you think the most important of these lessons was and show why you think it was most significant.
3. Contrast the parenting style of Louie's parents with the way other adults in the book dealt with either their children or with teenagers in general.
4. Describe the scene in the book that most stands out in your mind, now that you have finished it. Explain why you find that scene most memorable, both for your own life and as a reader.
5. Louie and Carter had very different reactions to the coach's order to get Washington out of the game, first before the game, then during and after it. Compare and contrast their views and discuss the ethics involved in both.

BOOKTALK IDEAS

1. Write the talk in the first person, letting Louie tell his own story.

2. Using the character description technique, have Carter describe Louie and his situation.
3. Focus your talk on the football team, training, the coach, and the scene when Louie quits and walks off the field.
4. Focus your talk on the relationship between Louie and Becky and how it helped him deal with the other things going on in his life.

📖 📖 📖

THE SHADOW BROTHERS. A. E. Cannon. Delacorte, 1990, 179p., $14.95. HS. Sociology, Psych, PE. Average; realistic fiction, romance.

SUBJECT AREAS
Minorities; Native Americans; Sports; Family relationships; Friendship; Rites of passage; School; Writing; Creativity; Self-knowledge.

CHARACTERS
Henry Yazzie: a Navajo teenager who has lived with the Jenkinses since he was 7. He is an athlete and a poet.

Marcus Jenkins: a 16-year-old who lives in his foster brother's shadow.

Mr. and Mrs. Jenkins: Marcus's parents and Henry's foster parents.

Julia Jenkins: Marcus's little sister.

Celia Cunningham: the best-looking girl in the school.

Diana Rogers: the Jenkinses' next-door neighbor.

Lennie Yazzie: Henry's father.

Frank: a Hopi who has a grudge against Henry.

BOOKTALK
Sometimes it seems as though I can still see him running, alone, late at night when he loved to run. Even if I never see him again, that image will stay in my mind, just like one of his

poems: "I weave through the night, run patterns in air, with the moon in my eyes and the stars in my hair."
That's a funny way for a guy to talk, you might say, but Henry was different. He came to live with us when he and I were both 7, just

after his mother died. His dad and my dad were best friends, and his dad didn't want him to go to the reservation school. Henry's smart, almost a genius. He's also a Navajo, but I never thought about that. He was just my brother. We did everything together, and I thought we always would.

This year. though, everything changed. First Henry started dating Celia, the school's major fox. Then he decided that he wanted to know more about being Navajo. He was different, and I didn't like it. I wanted the old Henry back. I wanted my brother back.

It wasn't until I tried to get him out of a fight at school and he hit me in the face and broke my nose that I finally realized the truth. The old Henry was gone forever, and I'd better start learning to get along without him.

What happened after that? Well, I think I'll just let you find that out yourself—about Lazarus, about Sutton and DeeDee, about Celia, and about what happened to Henry and what happened to me. (Adapted from a talk by Joni Richards Bodart in *Booktalk! 5*.)

MAJOR IDEAS OR THEMES
Finding your ethnic roots can help you understand yourself.

Brotherhood is as much emotional and psychological as it is biological.

Spending your life in another person's shadow can keep you from finding out who you really are, unless you leave and get out into the sunshine.

BOOK REPORT IDEAS
1. Describe how Henry's leaving helped Marcus.
2. Explain what Frank meant when he called Henry an "apple."
3. Compare how Henry felt about himself before and after he met Frank.
4. Speculate about what will happen in the fall. Will Henry come back? Why or why not?
5. Describe how the relationship between Marcus and Diana changed during the course of the book.
6. Discuss why running at night was so important to Henry. Marcus didn't understand it at first. Explain why not and what happened to help him understand.

BOOKTALK IDEAS
1. Center your talk around Henry, who he was and what he thought and the conflicts he had to deal with.
2. As Marcus, describe Henry and their relationship and what happened the year they were 16. (Be careful not to tell too much; end with a situation that will make someone else want to read the book.)
3. Describe one of the scenes of conflict between Marcus and Henry, leaving the ending unresolved.

4. Describe one of the scenes between Henry and Frank, showing the conflict between them.

📖 📖 📖

THE SILVER KISS. Annette Curtis Klause. Delacorte, 1990 198p., $14.95. HS. Eng, Psych. Quick read; supernatural, romance, adventure.

SUBJECT AREAS
Vampires; Death and dying; Friendship; Family relationships.

CHARACTERS
Zoe: a teenage girl who feels completely alone in the world.

Simon: a vampire with a conscience who preys only on small animals.

Lorraine: Zoe's best friend.

Mom: Zoe's mother, who is dying of cancer.

Dad: Zoe's father, who is preoccupied by his wife's illness.

Christopher: Simon's brother, an evil vampire.

BOOKTALK
Zoe felt as though everyone was leaving her. Her mother was dying of cancer, and her father was so concerned about his wife that he had all but forgotten he had a daughter. And now, Lorraine, her best friend, was moving to Oregon. She sat in the park in the shadowy darkness, thinking, "Soon I'll be all alone."

Just then she saw someone step out of the gazebo into the golden pool of light cast by a streetlight. He was slight, pale, with dark eyes and light, silvery hair. He was dressed completely in black. As she realized how beautiful he was, she started to cry. He saw her tears and fled, vanishing as silently as he'd appeared. Zoe was left alone, crying for all she had lost.

Simon couldn't stop thinking about the girl, how beautiful she was—dark like the night, pale, and thin, so very thin, almost as though one of his brethren had already claimed her. But no, she didn't have that smell about her. She was untouched. He was surprised to find himself thinking about her. He didn't usually think about people or want to talk to them. They were food, and one didn't talk to food. Still, he found himself wanting to see her again, to be with her, talk to her, maybe even kiss her—with the silver kiss, the one that would make her his forever.

So, on Halloween night, after the trick-or-treaters had come and gone, Zoe opened her front door and invited the real monster inside. (Adapted from a talk by Joni Richards Bodart in *Booktalk! 4.*)

MAJOR IDEAS OR THEMES

Evil exists and will grow and prosper if good does not fight it.

Love can transcend death.

Love is the ultimate gift and asks for nothing but love in return.

BOOK REPORT IDEAS

1. Discuss the differences between Simon and Christopher and why one was evil and one was not.
2. Describe what Zoe learns from Simon and how it changes her. What do you think happened after the book was over?
3. Discuss whether you would like to see a sequel to this book. Why or why not?
4. Describe the relationship between Zoe and her parents and tell how it changed and why.
5. Compare Christopher to other kinds of vampires, not necessarily super natural ones, that could exist in our world today.

BOOKTALK IDEAS

1. Write the talk in the first person from either Simon's or Zoe's point of view, leading up to how they discovered they were attracted to each other.

＊＊＊

SIMPLE GIFTS. Joanne Greenberg. Holt, Rinehart & Winston, 1986, 198p., $15.95. HS. Eng, Am Hist, Sociology. Thoughtful; humor, romance.

SUBJECT AREAS

Family relationships; History; Self-knowledge; Working; Substance abuse.

CHARACTERS

Mary Beth Fleuri: a big, loud, friendly woman who helps her husband and four children run a ranch.

Akin Fleuri: Mary Beth's husband. A thin, small, quiet man, he sleeps for 15 minutes every seven hours.

Robert Luther Fleuri: the oldest child and the only boy. He is the first to become interested in SCELP.

Kate Fleuri: Robert Luther's 15-year-old sister. She helps care for the younger girls.

Louise Fleuri: a 12-year-old who loves to read, daydream, and write poetry.

Jane Fleuri: the youngest, a 6-year-old who is more aware than the others realize.

Ralph Kelvin: the man from SCELP who recruits the Fleuris into the tourism program.

BOOKTALK

Hi! My name's Kate and I'm here to invite you to our ranch and tell you how our family got "perfect authenticity." To get to our ranch you have to ford two creeks and go halfway up a mountain on a road so rough it about shakes your car apart. But when you get to the top of the last rise, you can see our ranch, the house, the barn and corrals, and our fields. Mr. Kelvin had a fit the first time he saw it and wanted to sign us up in the SCELP program right away. That's a government program that helps people live like they were in another century so other folks can come visit and see what it was really like in the past. He wanted us to go back to 1880.

So we did, but we found out that it wasn't as easy living like pioneers as we'd thought it would be. You see, it was one thing to be authentic, it was another thing to be real—and Mr. Kelvin was always telling us how we couldn't be real because we had to make sure we were authentic. And some of the visitors we got weren't no picnic neither—especially that doctor's family that seemed bound and determined to find out all our secrets—like the way Daddy sleeps 15 minutes every seven hours, not like other folks, or the still that we had to hide—it was illegal even if it was real. And then there was the herd of longhorns Daddy kept up in one of the back pastures—they caused some problems, I guarantee you! But life's interesting, that's for sure. Come on up and see us, you hear, and we'll show you what the 1880s were *really* like!

(Adapted from a talk by Joni Richards Bodart in *Booktalk! 3.*)

MAJOR IDEAS OR THEMES

Authentic is not necessarily the same as real.

People have a tendency to judge others by how they look and act rather than what they are like inside.

Cooperating with the government can be a complicated business.

Knowledge can help people see the world more clearly, but too much knowledge too soon can rob children of their childhood.

Sometimes it takes a stranger to show you the value of familiar things.

Being too open with others can earn you their scorn instead of their friendship.

Take time out to appreciate what you have and who you are.

BOOK REPORT IDEAS
1. Discuss the idea of "real" versus "authentic" and the difference between the two ideas as they are seen in the book. If you could travel in time, which past would you see, the real one or the authentic one? Which would be easier for you to be, real or authentic, and why?
2. Discuss what you think the Fleuris learned from their trip back in time and how their lives will be different from now on. Explain who you think was changed the most and why.
3. Many people who knew the Fleuris laughed at them rather than trying to understand them. React to the idea that we judge others based solely on their appearance and actions and therefore never see the real person inside. This may be efficient, and sometimes necessary, but what are we missing out on? Include in your discussion how you might have reacted to the Fleuris had you been one of their neighbors.
4. This family worked together in both good and bad times. Show how that togetherness made their lives better and also more difficult.
5. Mary Beth was wise in her own way. Discuss several of her bits of wisdom or philosophy that show that she saw the world very clearly even when others didn't realize it.

BOOKTALK IDEAS
1. Make a poster or newspaper ad for SCELP and the chance to travel back to the 1880s, and use it as part of your talk or as an illustration of it.
2. Write your talk the way the book is written, letting several of the characters introduce themselves, speaking in the first person.
3. Focus your talk on the difference between what is real and what is authentic, and how the Fleuris had to learn the difference. Give several examples of both real and authentic, showing both the family's and the government's points of view.

🕮 🕮 🕮

TAKING TERRI MUELLER. Norma Fox Mazer. Avon, 1981, 192p., $2.75(pb); Morrow, 1983, 212p., $12.95. JH, HS. Eng, Psych. Average; realistic fiction, mystery.

SUBJECT AREAS
Kidnapping; Family relationships; Self-knowledge; Friendship; Ethics; Runaways.

CHARACTERS
Terri Mueller: a 13-year-old who lives with her father and believes her mother is dead.

Phil Mueller: Terri's father, who is a carpenter and handyman.

Vivian Mueller Eyes: Phil's older sister, who visits Phil and Terry once a year.

Kathryn Newhouse: Terri's mother, whom she has not seen for eight years.

Shaundra Smith: Terri's best friend.

Nancy Brief: a friend of Phil's whom he considers marrying.

Leif Brief: Nancy's 3-year-old son.

Grandmother Ethel and Grandfather Bob: Kathryn's parents and Terri's grandparents.

Merle Newhouse: Kathryn's husband and Terri's stepfather.

Leah Newhouse: Kathryn and Merle's 3-year-old daughter and Terri's half-sister.

BOOKTALK
Terri couldn't believe her ears. What did her aunt mean, "You have to tell Terri the truth—she's beginning to ask questions—she needs to know the truth!" The truth about what? The only questions she'd asked her aunt were about her mother, who had died when Terri was only 4. Or had she? What was the secret her father was unwilling to tell her? Was it something about her mother? About the reason Aunt Vivian was the only other relative she had? Or why she and her father moved so frequently, not staying anyplace more than six or eight months?

Terri had to know—and the answer might be in her father's locked box of papers. She knew he kept her birth certificate in there—maybe there was something else. There was—a divorce decree dissolving the marriage of Kathryn Susso Mueller and Philip James Mueller. But her parents weren't ever divorced! What's more, the paper was dated a year after her mother was killed. What did it mean? Could her mother be alive? And if she was, why had Terri's father lied to her for all those years?

MAJOR IDEAS OR THEMES
One's definition of morality governs one's actions.

Your ability to love someone may depend on whether you can accept or reject their actions based on your own definition of morality.

Understanding a person's reasons for doing something can help you forgive them.

The right choice is not always the easiest one.

In order to accept ourselves, we must first accept the totality of our past experiences.

We have to accept and deal with our past experiences, because we cannot change them.

Forgiveness frees us to see ourselves and the other person more clearly.

BOOK REPORT IDEAS
1. Debate the morality of Phil's actions, arguing first one side and then the other, basing your arguments on both the information in the book and your own moral and ethical standards.
2. Discuss Kathryn's reactions to Terri's first phone call, and later to Terri herself when she goes to visit Kathryn. How realistically are her emotions portrayed throughout the latter part of the book? If you think that they are not realistic, explain what you think a more realistic portrayal might have shown.
3. Discuss the morality of Terri's actions as she took increasingly more extreme measures to find out who and where her mother was.
4. Look at Terri's decision about which of her parents to live with, and explain why you think she made the decision she did. Base your answer not only on quotes from the book but also on your own understanding of Terri based on your own life experience.
5. Speculate on what you think happened after the end of the book, to Terri, to Phil, and to Kathryn and her new family.
6. Explain Vivian's actions based on your own understanding of her character as presented in the book.

BOOKTALK IDEAS
1. Use Terri's fragments of memory to show the audience what might have happened in the past, and relate some of her thoughts to the present.
2. Tell the story in the first person from Terri's point of view.

📖 📖 📖

TEX. S. E. Hinton. Dell, 1989, 191p., $3.25(pb); Delacorte, 1979, 224p., $13.95. JH, HS. Eng. Average; realistic fiction.

SUBJECT AREAS
Friendship; Family relationships; Rites of passage; Animals.

CHARACTERS
Tex McCormick: an easygoing, carefree 14-year-old who is ripe for getting into trouble.

Mason (Mace) McCormick: Tex's older brother, a super-straight 17-year-old who takes care of Tex while their father is away.

Pop: Tex and Mace's father, who travels most of the year with the rodeo.

Negrito: Tex's horse and one of his best friends.

Johnny Collins: Tex's best friend, who owns a dirt bike.

Bob Collins: Johnny's older brother and Mace's best friend.

Jamie Collins: Johnny and Bob's sister and the girl Tex loves.

Lem Peters: Mace's best friend before he married and moved to the city.

Cole Collins: the father of Johnny, Bob, and Jamie. He is a hard-nosed rich man who doesn't want his kids around the McCormick boys.

BOOKTALK
It all started when Mace sold their horses to get money to pay the gas bill and buy food. Tex swore he'd get Negrito back if it killed him, and they both lost their tempers. Tex would have scars from that fight for the rest of his life, both inside and out. It didn't help when their best friends' dad suddenly laid down the law about his sons not associating with Tex and Mace. Tex started getting into more trouble

than ever at school, and Mace worried more than he ever had—about Tex and about getting out of the little town where they lived. One of Mace's best friends had gotten a girl pregnant and had to get married, and Mace was determined not to let that happen to him. In fact, he didn't want any ties at all, and Tex figured that included him.

Then some things happened to change Tex's mind. First there was the big scene when their father came home. Then Tex and Mace were kidnapped by a crazed killer, and Tex and Johnny were nearly expelled from school. Finally, there was the night Tex watched Mace and Pop yell at each other, the night he heard Mace say the words that would change his life forever. "He's my brother even if he's not your son!"

Could Tex survive any more changes, any more losses? Or would he decide to just give up and go under for the last time?

MAJOR IDEAS OR THEMES

Some things just don't work out the way you want them too, and then you have to just do the best you can.

Sometimes you can understand why things happen, and sometimes you can't and just have to deal with them.

Whether you are a winner or a loser doesn't depend on how much money you have or how good-looking you are. It depends on who you are inside.

Love isn't just romance. It's sticking with someone every day, even when you'd rather be somewhere else.

Going too far, too soon, too fast can end up trapping you for life.

BOOK REPORT IDEAS

1. Compare the relationship between Mace and Tex at the beginning and at the end of the book.
2. Speculate on what you think happened after the book was over. For instance, did Mace go to college? How did Tex survive? What happened between him and Jamie? Give a rationale for each of your projections.
3. Discuss the part of the book that you feel most strongly about and explain why.
4. After Tex looked at the dead killer, he more or less forgot about it. Explain why he didn't have nightmares about it and Mace did.
5. Cole Collins didn't want his children around the McCormick boys. Explain why he felt that way and what, if anything, could make him change his mind.

BOOKTALK IDEAS

1. In the book, Tex tells the story. Try writing a booktalk that tells the story in the first person from Mace's point of view.

2. Focus your talk around the relationship between Tex and Mace.
3. Describe both Tex and Mace, and sketch in the conflict between them, leading up to a climax without telling the ending.
4. Tell about Tex and Mace from Johnny's point of view.

📖 📖 📖

THOSE SUMMER GIRLS I NEVER MET. Richard Peck. Dell, 1989, 177p., $2.95(pb); Delacorte, 1988, 177p., $14.95. JH. For Lang, Art, Eng. Quick read; realistic fiction, humor.

SUBJECT AREAS
Family relationships; Rites of passage; Aging; Death and dying; Travel.

CHARACTERS
Drew Wingate: a teen who has to cancel plans for his big sixteenth birthday party when his mother makes him take a cruise with his sister and grandmother.

Steph Wingate: Drew's 14-year-old sister.

Connie Carlson: Drew and Steph's grandmother, who used to be a famous torch singer.

Holly: a gorgeous English redhead who is the dance instructor on the cruise ship.

Shep: an old friend of Connie's, a piano player who drinks too much.

BOOKTALK
I heard my sister screaming as I walked up to the house. The whole neighborhood heard it—raw, 14-year-old rage. Mother had told her that there was no way out of it. We were going on a two-week cruise with our grandmother and a whole ship full of senior citizens. Steph didn't want to leave her friends, her Walkman, the mall, and MTV. I, on the other hand, had more serious problems. I would be turning 16 during those two weeks at sea, and my best friend would be getting his driver's license without me—not to mention the car we were sure his parents were going to give him for his birthday. Our birthdays were on the same day, and we'd been planning for months. Now it looked like all those plans were going in the toilet. No driver's license, no girls to impress with my new maturity—nothing except old folks, the open sea, and my bratty sister, who hated me.

But little did I realize what was waiting for me when I got on board. My grandmother, who used to be a torch singer, was not the kind of person I had expected at all. Then there was Holly, one of the dancers on board, who was tall, redheaded, and the most gorgeous thing I'd ever seen—until I met the other three women who danced with her. I may have missed my birthday on land, but I brought home a birthday present that would make not only my best friend but all the other guys at school really sit up and take notice!

MAJOR IDEAS OR THEMES
Thinking old and being old are two different things.

You may not know your family as well as you think you do.

People are not always who they seem to be.

Sometimes it is better to not tell all you know.

BOOK REPORT IDEAS
1. Explain why Connie invited Drew and Steph on the cruise.
2. Discuss how their image of their grandmother changed during the course of the voyage.
3. Discuss whether Drew and Steph will ever see their grandmother again, including your rationale for your belief.
4. Pretend you are either Drew or Steph and describe your voyage to either Bates or Gillian.
5. Describe how Drew and Steph see themselves at the beginning of the voyage and at the end of it.

BOOKTALK IDEAS
1. Describe the scene when Drew and Steph meet Connie for the first time; then explain how they ended up on a cruise for senior citizens.
2. Tell the story from Steph's point of view, perhaps as she told it to Melanie.
3. Contrast how Drew thought the cruise would be before and after he met Holly.
4. Use the relationship between Drew and Steph, perhaps conversations between them or their thoughts about each other, to tell the story.

📖 📖 📖

A VERY TOUCHY SUBJECT. Todd Strasser. Dell, 1986, 181p., $2.95(pb). HS. Sex Ed, Eng, Psych. Quick read; realistic fiction, humor, romance.

SUBJECT AREAS
Sex and sexuality; Friendship; Family relationships; Working; Substance abuse; Runaways.

CHARACTERS
Scott Tauscher: a 17-year-old who thinks about sex most of the time.

Alix Shaman: Scott's steady girlfriend, who is not interested in having sex yet.

Stu, Albert, and Gordy: Scott's best friends. Like him, they work as parking valets at the country club.

Mr. and Mrs. Tauscher: Scott's parents. He refers to them as Mr. Workaholic and Mrs. Activity.

Kerry Tauscher: Scott's 14-year-old sister, whose tennis playing could make her a teenage millionaire.

Paula Finkel: the Tauschers' neighbor who is determined to get her mother's attention.

Mrs. Finkel: Paula's alcoholic mother.

BOOKTALK
I'm Scott Tauscher, and I wrote this book because I and a lot of the guys I know have something in common when it comes to sex—it's been making us crazy for years. But don't think you're gonna be able to sit around with your friends and giggle at all the good parts—that's not why I wrote it. I'm 17 years old and have spent an average of 47 percent of my time over the past three years thinking and talking about sex.

But I decided to write a book about it because of something I saw almost every morning of the summer before my senior year in high school at about 8:15—I saw a guy leaving the house next door by climbing out of Paula's bedroom window. Paula Finkel is my next-door neighbor and is only 15 years old although you'd never know it from looking at her. Now I know that at 15, or even at 13, girls have sex—but you just don't expect it to be your next-door neighbor. Especially when Alix, who's the girl I've been going with for two years, won't let me get to first base.

But the action next door wasn't the only thing that happened that summer. It turned out to be full of unexpected surprises, like when my mother told me that I'd been conceived in a sleeping bag at a rock concert before my parents were married. Or like what happened when Alix left town for vacation and I got to know Paula, and what Alix did when she got back and found out about it. Or like what I heard when I really started listening to what the guys were saying when they talked about Paula—and about me!

MAJOR IDEAS OR THEMES
Sex and love are not the same.

Love can be expressed in many ways.

Losing your virginity is not something you do just to get it over with.

Thinking about sex and doing it are two different things.

Love is more important than sex in a relationship.

Self-control is more important than self-indulgence.

Your parents may not be the old fogies you think they are. You could be surprised!

BOOK REPORT IDEAS
1. Discuss what happened when Scott's parents found out about Paula and how they reacted. Compare that with how your parents might have reacted to the same situation.
2. At the end of the book, Scott's friends think his parents are going to be angry with him. Show why you think they were not.
3. Discuss why Paula didn't want to leave town. Explain why you think her reasons do or do not make sense.
4. Look at how Scott and Paula changed over the summer and how those changes will affect each of them in their individual lives in the future. In other words, what do you think happened after the end of the book?

BOOKTALK IDEAS
1. Use excerpts from the first three chapters of the book for your talk.
2. Tell the talk in the first person as if you were either Scott or Paula.
3. Find sentences or paragraphs that make you laugh or that make the book and the people in it real to you and use them as a basis for your booktalk.

📖 📖 📖

VOICES AFTER MIDNIGHT. Richard Peck. Dell, 1990, 181p., $3.50(pb); Delacorte, 1989, 181p., $14.95. JH. Eng, Am Hist. Quick read; supernatural, adventure.

SUBJECT AREAS
Time travel; Family relationships.

CHARACTERS

Chad: a 14-year-old Californian who goes to New York for two weeks with his family.

Heidi: Chad's older sister.

Luke: Chad's 8-year-old brother.

Melissa: Heidi's best friend.

Art: Luke's pug dog.

Emily and Tyler: a sister and brother who used to live in the town-house where Chad and his family are staying.

Mom and Dad: Chad, Heidi, and Luke's parents.

BOOKTALK

It was supposed to be a vacation—two weeks in New York while my dad reorganized his firm's Manhattan office. But it turned out to be something completely different. Dad rented this huge town-house for us to stay in, and my little brother Luke and I had the bed-rooms on the third floor. It started that first night when I woke up and heard voices, a boy and a girl. They were talking about how cold it was, and he was trying to reassure her. He kept saying he was sure they'd be rescued.

When I woke up again it was dawn, and I could see the cur-tains blowing in the wind. I got up and looked outside. The street was empty, no cars at all. A man stood in the street with a cart full of milk cans. As I watched, he poured some milk into a bucket and took it to the house next door. When I leaned out to see him better, I saw my sister Heidi sitting in her nightgown on our front steps. I couldn't be-lieve it—Heidi, outside in her nightgown, at dawn? I started to call her but then I realized how tired I was and just went back to bed.

Later I opened my eyes to bright daylight, and when I looked at the windows, I suddenly remembered—the house had central heat-ing and air conditioning. The windows were all nailed shut! Where—when—had I been?

Chad, Luke, and Heidi were in New York and in that town-house for a very specific reason. The whispering voices they could all hear grew weaker and weaker. They had to figure out what to do be-fore the voices died away completely, forever.

MAJOR IDEAS OR THEMES

Love can last even beyond death.

Everything happens for a reason.

The good that you do comes back to you.

By helping someone else, you may be able to help yourself.

Things that happened to our ancestors can have a direct influence on who we are today.

We are the sum total of everything that has happened to us in our lifetimes.

Even a small change can make a big difference.

BOOK REPORT IDEAS
1. Explain the significance of the golden cage with the telephone inside.
2. Explain how Heidi makes herself visible when she travels in time.
3. Discuss who first travels in time, including when and why.
4. Look at the ways that Chad's family was changed by their travels in time.
5. Show how Chad and Luke found the final clue that helped them rescue Tyler and Emily.
6. Explain Tyler's real identity—in other words, who he grew up to be.
7. Discuss the possibility of time travel and the changes you might make in your family if you could go back to the 1800s—but be careful who you kill off; they might be important later!

BOOKTALK IDEAS
1. Use the conversation between Tyler and Emily to either start or end your booktalk.
2. Tell the story from Heidi's or from Luke's point of view.
3. Use newspaper clippings from the great blizzard to illustrate your talk.
4. Center your talk around one of the trips the children make to the past.

📖 📖 📖

THE YEAR WITHOUT MICHAEL. Susan Pfeffer. Bantam, 1989, 176p., $2.95(pb); Bantam, 1988, 176p., $13.95. HS. Eng, Soc Studies. Thoughtful; realistic fiction, mystery.

SUBJECT AREAS
Runaways; Family relationships; Love; Friendship.

CHARACTERS

Michael Chapman: a ninth-grader who disappears on his way to a softball game at a friend's house.

Jody Chapman: Michael's older sister and the last family member to see him.

Kay Chapman: Michael and Jody's little sister.

Mr. and Mrs. Chapman: Michael, Jody, and Kay's parents, who are considering divorce.

Maris: a friend of Jody's who goes with her to a movie the day Michael disappears.

Jerry Murphy: the friend Michael is going to see when he disappears.

John Grainger: the detective hired to look for Michael.

BOOKTALK

It was the Sunday before Labor Day when Michael walked out the front door, promising me he wouldn't be late for dinner, and disappeared. That same Sunday our lives changed completely, irreversibly, and our family fell apart.

I'm Jody, and Michael's my little brother. I was the last person in our family to see him that day. Except for being concerned about the possibility that our parents would get a divorce, he seemed completely normal, not like someone who's about to drop out of sight. He didn't take his bike, and we don't even know if he took any money. We just know he never came back. He never got to do any of the things he'd planned to do once he got into high school. He was supposed to start ninth grade that week.

What would you do if your brother disappeared and your family fell apart and your friends got further and further away and everything just went crazy? I can only tell you how it was for me and my family that horrible year, the year I was a junior in high school—the year without Michael.

MAJOR IDEAS OR THEMES

In times of crisis a family can grow closer and stronger, or its members can turn against each other and be torn apart.

A crisis can exacerbate problems already present in a family.

Running away might seem like a solution for the person who leaves, but it can destroy the family that is left behind.

Avoiding a problem can make it worse.

Everyone must be allowed to express grief in their own way.

Grief goes through stages, from denial and anger to acceptance and recovery.

Sooner or later, you must deal with your grief and get on with your life.

BOOK REPORT IDEAS

1. Speculate on the reasons Michael left in the first place, particularly because, according to Jody, he didn't seem that upset when she talked with him that afternoon. What might have happened that we do not find out about in the book? One way you might do this is to write a letter, as Michael, to his family, explaining his disappearance.
2. There are definite stages of grief that people have to go through when dealing with a death or a loss in their lives. Show how these stages are portrayed in the book. (Elizabeth Kubler-Ross is a good source for information on these stages of grieving.)
3. Discuss how each family member tried to cope with Michael's disappearance and how well or how poorly those strategies worked.
4. Speculate on some of the other things that Michael might have tried to cope with the problems his family was having and how well they might or might not have worked.
5. Discuss whether Jody's trip to New York was a success or a failure.
6. Compare this family as the book opens and at its end—how has it changed and what have the various members learned during the year? What do you think will happen to them during the coming year, and how will they cope with it? Be sure to explain your reasons for your speculations.

BOOKTALK IDEAS

1. Write your talk in the first person as Jody.
2. Write your talk as if it were a news story or an announcement on a milk carton about a missing child.
3. Use a picture of a boy who looks like Michael to illustrate your talk.
4. Do a character sketch talk, describing each member of the family as they were when Michael left and posing the question, "How do you think these people will have to change to deal with Michael's disappearance?"
5. Write the talk as if you were a detective hired to solve the mystery of Michael's disappearance. Be sure you don't give too much of the plot away!

APPENDIXES
AND INDEXES

📖 APPENDIX A 📖

Tips for Writing
Effective Book Reports

1. Write down everything you will need to know about the assignment when the teacher tells you about it. Ask questions if you are not sure about something.

2. Go to the school or public library or a bookstore and get at least two or three books. Look in the library catalog for books on subjects you will like reading about or ask a librarian for help. Most bookstores have a subject arrangement. Ask one of the salespeople for help in finding the subject or subjects you are interested in. You should select more than one book in case you don't like the first one you picked out. It is very hard to enjoy reading or to write effectively about a book that you really don't like or that doesn't hold your attention.

3. Read a little bit every day and take notes on what you read as you go along. You need to jot down the characters' names and a brief description of each of them, a summary of the plot line, and any important scenes or ideas from the book (with the page numbers so you can find them again).

4. Try to plan a special time to read, and make sure you have something to take notes with and that you are not too tired. If you read when you're very tired, you might easily miss something important.

5. Organize your notes. Use a separate sheet for each topic in your book report, and keep them in order in one place so you will know where to find them. Putting them with the book is always a good idea.

6. Write your first draft using these four sections: a brief plot summary; the author's main idea or ideas, including why you think the author wrote the book; a discussion about the characters and the setting, with an evaluation of their realism and believability; and your own opinion of the book, why you either liked it or didn't like it, what kind of a person you think might like it, and to whom you would recommend it.

7. Check with your teacher to see if you are on the right track and doing what he or she expects you to do. Be sure to find out if you need to include any other information about the book or about the author.

8. Revise and edit your first draft. Check the spelling of all the words in your draft, and make sure that your grammar is also correct. At this point you may also want to change what you have written in the body of the report if you have thought of a better way to explain what you want to say or if you have thought of something else to add.

9. Make your final draft and proofread it to be sure there are no mistakes. Don't forget to put your name and class information on the top sheet, and if your paper is handwritten be sure that your writing is clear and easy to read.

10. Turn in your paper on the due date.

These ideas are partially based on *Scholastic's A + Junior Guide to Book Reports* by Louise Colligan (Scholastic, 1989, $2.50), which has much more information and also helpful forms in it that you can use to make sure that your book reports are easier to write and easier to make an A on.

📖 APPENDIX B 📖

Tips for Writing
Effective Booktalks

1. A booktalk is not a book report but a kind of commercial for a book that persuades the listener to read it. Therefore, it doesn't tell the ending and doesn't evaluate the book in any way. It just tells a little about the plot and the characters and stops without telling what happened next.

In addition, a book report is mainly something that you write and the teacher reads (although you may be asked to read it in class as well), but a booktalk is usually spoken. It is really talking about the book. It is basically the kind of thing you'd say to a friend when you've just finished a book you really liked and want to make sure that your friend reads it too.

2. Never talk about a book that you didn't like—how could you convince someone else to read it if you didn't like it?

3. Never talk about a book you haven't read all the way through—you might miss something crucial, or your teacher might ask you to talk with him or her privately about the end of the book.

4. There are four basic kinds of booktalks, based on what you thought was exciting in the book.

Plot summary is the first kind. You just summarize the plot, leading up to an exciting and climactic moment and stopping without telling what happened. The last sentence for a talk like this could be "To find out what happened next, read. . . ." Make sure you don't tell too much of the book. A rule of thumb is that you never tell more than 25 percent of the book, and sometimes you can tell a lot less!

Character description is another kind of booktalk, one that is based on talking about one or two or more of the main characters in the book. You can pretend that you are one of the characters and write your talk in the first person, or you can just describe the characters in the third person. The more characters you use, the less you can say about each one of them, because you don't want to make your talk too long.

If you are writing about a book that is a collection of short stories or is written in an episodic style (the main character might have a series of adventures or problems to deal with, each one contained in one or two chapters), you can use the short story/scene kind of booktalk. This talk simply tells the whole story or scene (or one adventure or problem) from beginning to end. The last few sentences of the talk let the audience know that there are other adventures or stories that they will miss if they don't read the book.

If the author of your book has a unique writing style or if the book itself has a mood about it—mysterious, scary, or suspenseful—then you will want to write a mood-based booktalk. This kind of talk lets your audience know what to expect from the book and sometimes includes an excerpt from it that demonstrates the author's writing style. In order to communicate the mood, you'll need to use your voice, including variations in pitch, pace, and rhythm, to convey the mood.

5. A booktalk shouldn't be too long; it usually lasts between two and five minutes, depending on how much of the book you have to tell to convince your audience to read it. This means that you will have to leave out either most or all of the details about the book and just put into your talk what is absolutely necessary.

6. Take notes while you read your book, including the names of the characters and the page number of any special scene or quote you want to use in your talk.

7. Make your first sentence exciting so that it will hook your audience immediately. Start in the middle of the action, and be sure to include more action than description, because most audiences find action more interesting. Once you have gotten your audience's attention with your first sentence, they will be more willing to listen to what else you have to say.

8. Time your talk after you've written it, while you are practicing, to make sure that it isn't too long. Be sure that you do practice and that you practice not only what you are going to say but also the way you're going to stand, how you will handle the book itself and your notes on it, and whatever gestures you will use. If you don't practice everything at once, you will be more likely to forget something you really wanted to say when you deliver your talk. Make sure you also practice projecting your voice so everyone in the room can hear you.

9. Don't memorize your talk! Use slightly different words when you practice so that if you forget the exact words you have written down, you will have some other familiar words to fill in. This means that you shouldn't look at your notes too much while you practice after the first two or three times you read it aloud. This will force you to find different words to use.

10. Wear comfortable clothes. I always make sure that I have pockets in my skirt or pants so I have somewhere to put my hands to keep

from waving them around. And remember to speak slowly, because you may be nervous and more likely to speed up without realizing it. But most of all, remember to have fun! That's one of the main purposes of booktalks—to have fun sharing books you've enjoyed with other people who will enjoy them too.

And there's also an extra bonus to doing booktalks. People are more afraid of getting up in front of a crowd and talking than anything else. If you learn how to do this, while you are learning how to give booktalks, you'll have an advantage over all of them!

There is more information about how to write and present booktalks in my book *Booktalk! 2* (H. W. Wilson, 1985, $32.00). Most public and school libraries have copies of this book. In addition, your librarians may be willing to share their own hints on how to do booktalks.

📖 APPENDIX C 📖

Recent Titles Popular with Teens

These reviews are reprinted from the well-known magazine *Voice of Youth Advocates (VOYA)*. This magazine is published for librarians who select the books libraries buy for their young adult collections. The date of the issue in which the review appears is at the bottom of each description. Each book is also rated by the reviewer on a scale of 1 to 5 (5 is the best) for quality of writing (Q) and interest or popularity (P). A rating of 5Q 5P would be the best—top quality and most interesting for teens.

THINNEST

SEEDFOLKS. Paul Fleischman. HarperCollins, 1997, 69p., $13.95.

In the narrative style of Fleischman's *Bull Run* (HarperCollins, 1993) or Carolyn Meyer's *Rio Grande Stories* (Harcourt, 1994) the voices of Cleveland's Gibbs Street neighborhood are revealed chapter by chapter. Their focus is a garbage-laden, vacant lot that grows into a well-tended garden for the inner-city, multiethnic characters who might otherwise never become involved with one another. Insights into cultures and individuals are simply drawn: a British nurse recalls "ancient Egyptians prescribed walking through a garden as a cure for the mad;" a Korean dry cleaner recovers from a robbery attack through his experiences in the garden; Macho Curtis, also known as "Biceps R Us," plants tomatoes to impress his lost love Lateesha; and Maricela, a pregnant teen, learns the value of life through her garden experience.

Wise, entertaining sketches make this an ideal choice for crossover lists, reluctant readers, and multicultural studies.

June 1997
Scores: 4Q 4P

WHISTLE ME HOME. Barbara Wersba. Henry Holt, 1997, 108p., $14.95.

Noli, seventeen, is amazed when TJ, a new boy at school, chooses her to be his girlfriend. During their five-month involvement, TJ is the perfect soulmate, but Noli can't understand why he doesn't seem to want a sexual relationship with her. One night, after a brief attempt at physical intimacy, Noli realizes TJ is gay. When he admits he always has been that way but was trying to change himself, Noli flies into a rage. In the weeks that follow, Noli is numb with grief and her problem drinking becomes worse. She is forced to join AA and manages to quit drinking, start new friendships, and move toward healing her damaged relationship with her mother. Noli refuses TJ's attempt at platonic friendship, realizing she needs more time to heal.

In the end, Noli begins to forgive TJ, believing she might love again, and TJ is happy with a new boyfriend.

These characters are three-dimensional. Noli is likeable, though given to cruel, angry outbursts. Teens will relate to her experience of falling in love and being hurt, the overwhelming joy and the sharp disappointment. TJ is an interesting character—excelling at everything but being true to himself. His struggles for self-acceptance and his grief over the loss of his friendship with Noli will touch readers. It is easy to empathize with both characters' dilemma, which is why this book is so worthwhile. The beautiful cover photograph of two teens walking in the woods reflects the emotional tone of the story. This brief, well-written novel deals sensitively with important issues.

August 1997
Scores: 4Q 4P

THINNER

BURIED ONIONS. Gary Soto. Harcourt Brace, 1997, 160p., $17.00.

Eddie is a nineteen-year-old Hispanic city college dropout trying to make good on his own in Fresno, California. Everyday Eddie is faced with death: his father's, his cousin's, and the threat of his own. He sees the city he lives in as being built over a huge onion, "that remarkable bulb of sadness" that makes strong men like him cry.

He tries to separate his own identity from the violent nature and stupidity he sees in his comrades, but he cannot seem to avoid danger. Eddie gets a job landscaping for a trusting man, but when someone from his community steals the employer's truck, Eddie is too ashamed to go back and admit what happened. He lies low and avoids the phone. While contemplating his future employment, Eddie begins to suspect that his cousin—who was sliced open with a rough, dirty blade—was murdered by his best friend, and Eddie feels his own life might be in danger. In an action-packed second half, Eddie dodges through the dirty barrio, trying to avoid the suspected killer while also experimenting with ways to escape his neighborhood.

Soto has created a beautiful, touching, and truthful story about one young man struggling to keep his dignity and not bend to the will of the glue-sniffing locals. Much like the modern classic film *Boyz in the Hood*, this story, which resorts to neither stereotypes nor cliches, portrays a young man fighting against society to make a place for himself in the world.

The lyrical language and Spanish phrases add to the immediacy of setting and to the sensitivity the author brings to his character's life. *Buried Onions* is Soto's best fiction yet. Especially recommended to teen readers who enjoyed Walter Dean Myers's *Scorpions* (Harper, 1988) or Jess Mowry's *Way Past Cool* (Farrar, 1992).

October 1997
Scores: 5Q 4P

CLOCKWORK. Philip Pullman. Arthur A. Levine/Scholastic, 1998, 128p., $16.95.

A group of villagers gather in a tavern in a small German town on the night before Karl, apprentice to the clockmaker Herr Ringelmann, is to reveal his new figure of the great clock of the Glockenheim. What the villagers and Herr Ringelmann do not know is that Karl has been unable to create a figure for the clock and he is in the depths of despair. Karl confides his secret to Fritz, the novelist who has come to share his newest story, but Fritz has problems of his own—he has not finished his story, and he has no idea how it will end. His tale of a young prince and Dr. Kalmenius, a maker of clockworks, takes a sudden twist when Dr. Kalmenius appears in the inn. Fritz flees in fear when it appears that his story has come to life and fit Karl, serving girl Gretl, and the great clock into its components as neatly, relentlessly, and steadily as well oiled clockwork.

This is a dark, neat, and nifty tale that is accessible to younger readers but should also attract older fantasy readers, particularly fans of Pullman's still unfinished *Dark Materials* trilogy (the two books published so far are *The Golden Compass* and *The Subtle Knife*).

The tale is seamless, resolving happily and convincingly, with both the good and brave and the craven and cowardly receiving appropriate rewards. Pullman laces his tale with subtle humor while maintaining the suspense until the end. Misty, moody, and atmospheric black-and-white drawings by Leonid Gore make a perfect setting for this gothic gem.

December 1998
Scores: 5Q 4P

HEROES. Robert Cormier. Delacorte, 1998, 135p., $15.95.

Eighteen-year-old Francis Joseph Cassavant returns to Frenchtown, hideously wounded after falling on a grenade in World War II. His face has been destroyed and he awaits reconstructive surgery that may not be successful. Cormier's dark, mysterious style projects a sense of impending doom, and the reader soon learns that Francis has returned in order to carry out a mission involving the talented, handsome founder of Frenchtown's recreation program, Larry LaSalle, and Francis's young girlfriend, Nicole Renard. LaSalle, already considered a hero for his dedication to the town's youth, has earned a Silver Star for bravery at Guadalcanal.

Through flashback, Cormier reveals that it was Larry LaSalle who helped Francis overcome his shyness and gave him the self-confidence to win the love of beautiful Nicole. However, Larry, the shining hero, is a tragically flawed human being. After a party celebrating his heroic return from the war, Larry rapes Nicole, and Francis, hiding nearby, is too frightened to intervene. Overwhelmed by guilt and shame, Francis fakes his birth certificate, enlists in the Army, and finally attempts suicide by falling on a grenade. This desperate act saves the lives of his company and earns Francis a Silver Star.

Cormier explores the meaning of heroism and the hidden motivations for what may appear to be heroic acts. Teens will understand Francis's adulation of Larry, who helped realize his potential and then his bitter feelings of betrayal when Francis learns the truth about his idol. The theme of guilt and revenge is also powerful and readers will identify with Francis's final desperate attempt to assuage his guilt by killing Larry LaSalle. But when the two "heroes" finally come face to face with each other after years of war, death, and despair, the answer is not so simple. Once again, Cormier has written a suspenseful novel that addresses serious questions of concern to most young adults.

August 1998
Scores: 5Q 4P

NO MAN'S LAND: A YOUNG SOLDIER'S STORY. Susan Bartoletti. Blue Sky/Scholastic, 1999, 169p., $15.95.

In a thrilling opening scene, fourteen-year-old Thrasher and his father are hunting alligators in their Georgia swamp when a female alligator attacks Pap. Frightened, Thrasher stands "transfixed, his feet planted as if mired in mud." Neighbors rescue the pair, but Thrasher feels weak and unmanly because of his response. His mother is sympathetic, but knows his father is disappointed. Thrasher joins the Confederate Okefenokee Rifles by lying about his age. Life in the army is not very exciting and he longs for a battle to prove that he is brave. Eventually, he is in the Battle of Gaines' Mill, and proves his courage, though with an unexpected outcome.

Although there are several exciting scenes, much of the book is introspective. As Thrasher matures, his experiences teach him about manhood and bravery. He finds out that Tim, a soldier, is a girl, and wonders why a girl would want to be in the war. The answer comes through a letter of Tim's that is read after Tim's death. There is a bibliography for further reading and an epilogue that states that the characters are fictional, but the experiences are based on facts.

December 1999
Scores: 3Q 3P

THE REVELATION OF SAINT BRUCE. Tres Semour. Orchard, 1998, 128p., $16.95.

Bruce is not a saint and resents the fact that his friends choose to see him as one. It is difficult for him to be involved in impure activities, though. When his friend hits the jackpot at a telephone booth, Bruce feels guilty even considering eating the pizza that is bought with the money, believing that the money belongs to the telephone company. Bruce refuses to conform to typical high school rituals such as pep rallies, which he dodges by convincing a teacher to sponsor him and his friends so they can study instead of cheering for an athletic team. When Bruce is out sick and the sponsoring teacher is also absent, his friends drink a bottle of Jack Daniels in the classroom. They tell Bruce, and when confronted by the teacher Bruce cannot tell a lie and gets his friends into serious trouble. Bruce is blamed by his friends, but he contemplates whether he should be at fault since they are the guilty ones.

Life becomes difficult for Bruce as his friends become his enemies. Nevertheless, Bruce remains independent, sometimes questioning his actions but overall knowing that he had no choice in telling the truth. A Bible quotation begins each chapter. The story is thought-provoking, especially regarding the academic vs. athletic theme. The students make the most sense, realizing that studying is a better use of time. Drinking Jack Daniels shows that they are only human and although they had good intentions, they could not resist temptation. The author's voice sounds convincingly like a teenager, and the central dilemma—loyalty to friends vs. personal ethics and morality—is one that many teens may find themselves confronting.

February 1999
Scores: 5Q 4P

TOUGHING IT. Nancy Springer. Harcourt Brace, 1994, 140p., $10.95 hc, $4.95 pb.

Sixteen-year-old Shawn Lacey, better known as Tuff, is riding passenger on his older brother Dillon's mountain bike when a shotgun blast from a rigged booby trap instantly kills Dillon. Tuff is thrown into shock and is barely coherent as he runs for help. Then he must confront his alcoholic mother, a woman mired in poverty with five additional children by an abusive husband, who seems unable to grasp that her oldest child is dead, and when she does, mutters something about Dillon being better off. For all their lives Dillon and Tuff have fantasized about finding their father, whose identity their mother refuses to reveal. But, as Tuff makes his decision to leave home, his mother says "go and find Pen Leppo—he's your father." Tuff's only goal is to find Dillon's murderer and kill him. He finds Pen, whose steady understanding alters what might have been a tragic outcome.

Sprinter has captured the rage that the victims of senseless violence can feel, rage that can destroy them if not derailed. She also offers a wonderful portrait in Pen of an older man mentoring a youth in trouble. None of this is done in a preachy manner, but follows the natural development of the characters.

August 1994
Scores: 4Q 5P

VANISHING. Bruce Brooks. HarperCollins, 1999, 160p., $14.95.

Alice, eleven years old, has no control over the breakup of her parents or how it will affect her. Although she wants to live with her father, he sends her home ill to live with her alcoholic mother and a new stepfather who dislikes her. While hospitalized for bronchitis, Alice stops eating. As her weight decreases, she begins to enjoy the lightheaded—but very clear—feeling that her body is hovering between the ceiling and the bed. Her heightened sense makes her aware of being totally in charge. As long as she refuses to eat, she cannot be forced to leave the hospital. Only her friendship with Rex, a dying patient, keeps her anchored to life.

Brooks, no stranger to the young adult audience, has written a powerful novel that addresses several themes, including the concerns faced by children of divorce. Alice feels betrayed by her father and abandoned by her alcoholic mother. The impact of not feeling loved or valued is overwhelming, coaxing her to crave increasing hallucinations, even at the risk of coma and inevitable death. The reader is reminded that there is always someone who cares. In this story, it is a dying boy who offers a wise lesson: "All you get by giving up is 'The Big Nothing.'"

October 1999
Scores: 5Q 3P

THIN

BAD. Jean Ferris. Farrar, Straus & Giroux, 1998, 192p., $16.00.

Sixteen-year-old Dallas craves excitement—a craving that leads to her arrest for the armed robbery of a convenience store. Deserted by her friends and accomplices and given up on by her disappointed father, Dallas is sentenced to six months in the Girls' Rehabilitation Center. There she encounters an assortment of other "bad" girls, some trying to turn their lives around, others not certain they can change or that they even want to.

These girls are from a variety of backgrounds—some poor, some middle class, and one wealthy girl who views her time at the Center as a "vacation." Many of the girls have been victims of abuse and neglect, and are struggling to understand the concept of being responsible for their own actions despite what their friends and families may do. Dallas benefits from watching some of the repeat offenders revert to their old ways once on the "outside," and a few who manage to alter their behavior. A kindly counselor introduces Dallas to books such as Carson McCullers's *The Heart is a Lonely Hunter* (Bantam, 1983, @1940) that help Dallas to break out of her own self-absorbed shell.

Ferris conducted series of interviews with inmates in a rehabilitation center in preparation for writing *BAD*. The voices of Dallas, the other girls, and the counselors ring true and readers will relate to Dallas's search for self amidst unsavory circumstances. An insightful and non-judgmental novel, this is also an absorbing quick read that should appeal to many young adults.

February 1999
Scores: 5Q 4P

MAX THE MIGHTY. Rodman Philbrick. Blue Sky, 1998. 176p., $16.95.
    This sequel to *FREAK THE MIGHTY* (Scholastic, 1998/*VOYA* April 1994) continues the exploits of Maxwell Kane, the young "giant-of-a-boy" who befriends other outcasts and slays imaginary dragons in the form of real-life problems. Max narrates this story of twelve-year-old Rachel, a junior high classmate who relies on him for help. Rachel, nicknamed Worm by other kids because she is constantly reading, has been living inside books to escape from her abusive stepfather, the "Undertaker." Max witnesses Rachel and her mother's fear when they are caught by the Undertaker in the park, follows them home, and rescues Rachel.
    The Undertaker accuses Max of kidnapping, and Max and Rachel run away to find her father in Chivalry, Montana. Rachel is running away from her present and Max from his past. They have various adventures on the road-hitched rides on psychedelic buses and hopped fright cars; and encounter numerous characters, both helpful and not. Attacks by guard dogs, the "Hippy Dippy" Hobo Joe, and police chases confront them on their way. The secret of Rachel's father is revealed in Chivalry and the resulting climax is dangerous, exciting, and enlightening. Though not quite as good as *Freak*, this is a worthy sequel and provides some excellent comments on the value of reading.

June 1998
Scores: 4Q 4P

THE MUSIC OF DOLPHINS. Karen Hesse. Scholastic Press, 1996, 196p., $14.95.
    Following her rescue by the Coast Guard, researchers discover that Mila has been raised by dolphins, and attempt to rehabilitate her to the human world. But in their zeal to study and learn from her, they imprison and threaten to destroy the special connection to another world that makes her unique.
    A profound study of being human and the ways in which communication unites and separates living beings, Hesse's prose poem combines an intriguing format and typeface that Mila's development and growing sociability, as it contrasts with the isolation and fear of another feral child, Shay. With an almost dreamlike style, Mila ponders the differences between her island home and dolphin family and the house she shares with the doctors. Even while she rapidly grasps the use of computers and becomes enthralled with making music, Mila finds herself drawn back to the sea and a more elemental way of life than civilization can offer.

Mila's rich inner voice makes her a lovely, lyrical character. The idea of a "wild child" with an adolescent's questions and yearnings is appealing and the seemingly simplicity of the storyline belies the complex technique. But with the *in medias res* opening, the preponderance of interior monologue and sophisticated styles, this will probably not be a first choice for reluctant readers.

August 1998
Scores: 5Q 3P

THE SACRIFICE. Diane Matcheck. Farrar, Straus & Giroux, 1998, 224p., $16.00.

Weak-one-who-does-not-last prides herself on being nothing like the other Apsaalooka (Crow) girls. She is determined to become a warrior despite her father's and the rest of the tribe's wishes, and she is determined to prove that she, not her twin brother, who dies at age four, is the "Great One" her father envisioned before their births. Seizing the opportunity to prove herself to the tribe, Weak-one disobeys when she is forbidden to go with the war party to avenge her father's death.

Not always a likeable character, Weak-one is often self-centered and angry, but she is also brave and resourceful—characteristics that see her through several close encounters with death when she loses the war party's trail. Weak-one survives being scalded by a geyser and attacked by a bear before she is captured by a band of Pawnee. At the Pawnee camp, Weak-one is befriended by Wolfstar, and through him she learns true friendship and trust. Readers watch as Weak-one grows from a self-centered girl to a strong, courageous young woman as she overcomes one obstacle after another.

Weak-one is a complex and interesting character, but the plot is the driving force behind the book. Matcheck keeps the reader wondering how Weak-one will survive to prove that she is indeed the Great One until the very end. Good characterization coupled with a tight plot and authentic setting make this book a good choice not only for readers interested in early Native American life but also for readers looking for a good coming-of-age or adventure story.

February 1999
Scores: 4Q 4P

THE TERRORIST. Caroline B. Cooney. Scholastic, 1997, 208p., $15.95.

Sixth-grader Billy Williams is a typical American boy living in London with his family for a year. His sister Laura is also a typical American kid—little interested in world events or scholastic endeavors. When Billy is the victim of a terrorist's bomb, however, she is horrified and immediately focuses on finding his killer, filtering her search through classmates, a cosmopolitan group from all over the world. One of them, an Iranian girl named Jehran, begins to beg Laura to sell her Billy's passport. As Laura learns more about terrorists and their causes, she also is drawn into Jehran's plan to gain entry into the United States to avoid an arranged marriage. While Laura tries to help Jehran and makes arrangements for her to fly to New York, she also is suspicious of Jehran's story. At the last minute, her suspicions over-rule her heart, and Laura foils Jehran's plan to enter the United States illegally.

Cooney's works are almost always popular with teens, and this one will be, too. The characterizations are well done, the terrorist bombing is taken from today's headlines, and the setting is exotic enough to add to the mystery, but familiar enough to seem real to the reader. The fact that a youngster dies and his family is left to handle their grief with no real answers is tragic and ambiguous yet realis-tic—there are few definite answers in acts of terrorism. Cooney has another winner to add to her long list.

October 1997
Scores: 4Q 4P

📖 AUTHOR INDEX 📖

📖 TITLE INDEX 📖

CURRICULUM AREA INDEX

This index contains a more comprehensive listing of curriculum areas than is listed in each entry.

Ethics

📖 GENRE INDEX 📖

This index contains a more comprehensive listing of genres
than is listed in each entry.

📖 READABILITY INDEX 📖

📖 SUBJECT INDEX 📖

This index contains a more comprehensive listiug of subject
areas than is listed in each entry.

Death and Dying
See also **Aging; Illness, Mental and Physical; Suicide**

Dinosaurs
See also **Animals**

Divorce
See also **Adoption; Family Relationships; Stepparents**

Eating Disorders
See also **Illness, Mental and Physical**

End-of-the World Scenarios

Environment

**Self-Knowledge/
Self-identity**

Sex and Sexuality

📖 ABOUT THE AUTHOR 📖

Known nationally as an author, lecturer, and workshop leader on booktalking and young adult literature, Joni Richards Bodart has been active in the ALA Young Adult Library Services Association since the 1970s. Formerly assistant professor at Emporia State University in Kansas, she is now on the faculty of the University of Denver's Department of Library and Information Services. She holds a doctorate in library science and a second master's in psychology. She lives in Colorado, where in addition to teaching, she works as a writer and consultant on YA services, and as a part-time reference/young adult librarian for Denver Public Library.

3/1160 1535 7376